ue

D0074822

WITHDRAWN

How to Build a
Conscious Machine

Alden
128.2
An43h

How to Build
a Conscious Machine

Leonard Angel

Westview Press
BOULDER, SAN FRANCISCO & LONDON

All rights reserved. No part of this publication may be reproduced or transmitted in any form or by any means, electronic or mechanical, including photocopy, recording, or any information storage and retrieval system, without permission in writing from the publisher.

Copyright © 1989 by Leonard Angel

Published in 1989 in the United States of America by Westview Press, Inc., 5500 Central Avenue, Boulder, Colorado 80301, and in the United Kingdom by Westview Press, Inc., 13 Brunswick Centre, London WC1N 1AF, England

Library of Congress Cataloging-in-Publication Data
Angel, Leonard, 1945–
   How to build a conscious machine / by Leonard Angel.
     p. cm.
   Bibliography: p.
   ISBN 0-8133-0944-1
   1. Mind and body.   2. Consciousness.   3. Artificial intelligence.
   1. Title.
   BF161.A63   1989
   128′.2—dc20

                                               89-32693
                                             CIP

Printed and bound in the United States of America

The paper used in this publication meets the requirements of the American National Standard for Permanence of Paper for Printed Library Materials Z39.48-1984.

10   9   8   7   6   5   4   3   2   1

Contents

ALLEGHENY COLLEGE LIBRARY

90-4648

CAT Feb 4 '91

12-19-90 mK 40.99 Alden

Acknowledgments

This book has been a number of years in the making, and it would be impossible to thank everyone with whom I have discussed matters of mind and machine and from whom I have undoubtedly benefited. Amongst my colleagues at the University of British Columbia, I would particularly like to thank Sam Coval, Tom Patton, Earl Winkler, and Mark Glouberman of the Philosophy Department, as well as Richard Rosenberg of Computer Science and Guy Carden of Linguistics, for providing helpful comments and directions concerning various aspects of the manuscript or whole drafts of it. I'm indebted as well to Bob Bunn, Dale Beyerstein, Ed Levy, Claudia Casper, Bob Hadley, Ali Kazmi, Gary Wedeking, Jeff Foss, David Perlmutter, Peter Apostole, Kurt Preinsperg, Ronnie de Sousa, George Levy and Peter Remnant for discussions, encouragements, and research help. Michael Feld was especially encouraging and helpful with various drafts of the work. Lionel Kearns and Jerri Sinclair provided the right support at the right time. I'd also like to thank both Jim Anderson for steering me in the direction of Westview Press, and my editor at Westview, Spencer Carr, for his generous assistance with the manuscript and final revisions. Thanks are due to Libby Barstow and Chris Arden for their thorough copy editing, and to Olga Betts for final manuscript preparation. Louise Schmidt has been truly generous with her time and energy in the preparation of the manuscript, and of real assistance with her comments as well. I'd also like to thank the anonymous readers for their insights and suggestions. And, finally, thanks to Susan for her patience and support.

Introduction

In the characters of Pygmalion, the Golem, Frankenstein, Pinocchio, HAL, and many others, our story tellers have conceived of building something which turns out to be conscious. Only in this century, however, can we begin to entertain the project of actually building such a thing. To some, such a project seems distasteful or morally dangerous. To others, it looms ahead as the most exciting scientific venture of all, the culmination of 2,600 years of physics, philosophy, psychology, and engineering. To others still, it is a project with little or no prospect of success. In this book I take both the project and skepticism concerning its feasibility as seriously as they can be taken. Can it be done? Can we build a conscious, self-reflective machine?

To begin with, I suggest we must distinguish between the task of constructing a machine that *seems* to have consciousness, on the one hand, and the task of deciding whether it *in fact* has consciousness, on the other. Success in the first enterprise depends on our ability to build things that pass ever more sophisticated tests. But no matter how many tests such devices pass, an assessment of whether they really have consciousness depends on one's view of the relationship between the behavior a thing engages in and the having of consciousness. Two examiners might agree on whether some device manages to pass a specified battery of tests but disagree on whether the passing of those tests is a warrant for the conclusion that the device is really conscious.

Skeptics about the ambition of artificial intelligence (AI) practitioners to build a conscious machine, then, arrive from two directions: There are those who think we won't be able to build a machine that so much as seems conscious, and there are those who believe that no matter how many behavioral tests a device passes, no matter how much a mere machine seems to be conscious, it would not really be conscious.

This book attempts to address both the engineering issue and the philosophical issue, as I'm calling them. On the first question, Will we be able to construct a machine that at least seems to be conscious? I am advancing a highly optimistic thesis. I suggest that we are already in a position to build a rational agent that inhabits an environment, has

ix

survival strategies with respect to its environment, has the ability to identify other elements of its environment as rational agents, and has the ability to learn from the human agents it has so identified a significant amount of the humans' language. Moreover, it will not include any conventional elements of the humans' language as part of its innate program. And it will use the language in conversation with humans in a rational way — that is, as an instrument in the satisfaction of its purposes and the purposes of its interlocutor. In other words, we are already in a position to build an independently purposive simple language-learning and language-using machine. To show that this is so, I present the master design of such a device.

As the reader familiar with the literature will see, this design includes the first sketch of a program for pure or natural interagency attribution, as well as the first attempt to design a 'pure language-acquisition device' — that is, a language-learning program that in its initial state contains no conventional elements. My claim is that what I call 'pure interagency attribution' is the one essential element of rational agency that has thus far been ignored by AI theoreticians. As a result of this gap, the area has been baffled by frame, mentality, and integration problems that are not as intractable as they have seemed. In fact, these problems are not intractable at all but, rather, are capable of clear and definite theoretical solutions. Once we have seen the fundamental nature of pure or natural interagency attribution, and have constructed devices that embody such competences, the foundation has been laid for the design of entirely natural language-acquisition models.

If this master design is sound, there is at present no reason to think that such devices are not indefinitely elaborable. There is no reason to think that we cannot indefinitely complexify so as to arrive at remarkably humanoid androids. The project, then, even to the limited extent the master design is carried out here, is ambitious.

In order to demonstrate the viability of the engineering project of Part 1, I present first (Chapter 1) the philosopher's specifications to the cognitive-scientist-cum-engineer as to what will count as a primitive android. Following this (Chapters 2 and 3) is the cognitive-scientist-cum-engineer's master design in response to these specifications. The nonspecialist reader will not be too shocked, I hope, to discover that the exposition of the master design includes many technical details that are pitched to the specialist. I have, however, taken pains to expose the master design with as little jargon as possible and to keep the narrative outlines as smooth as possible, so that even the nonspecialist reader will be able to follow the central features of the design.

By the end of Part 1, then, we have followed the design of a primitive language-learning, language-using android, and we have seen reason to hold that there may well be a research continuum between the primitive language-learning and language-using android, on the one hand, and the more fully humanoid android, on the other. In any case, the fairly primitive language-learning, language-using androids would seem a good deal more conscious than anything we have today. So if our question is, "Will we be able to build machines that seem conscious on stringent behavioral tests?" our answer is "Very likely."

Now there are some philosophers who argue that for something to be conscious is nothing other than for it to embody the design of a sufficiently complex rational agent. An entity that embodies the design of rational agency, and therefore gives the appearance of being conscious, *is* conscious; or at least it would be mere programmatic agnosticism to refuse to ascribe to it real consciousness as opposed to mere apparent consciousness. (See, for example, Dennett 1978a.) On the other hand, there are those philosophers who argue that embodiment of the design of rational agency is not in itself sufficient for the having of consciousness. In addition to behaving in the apparently conscious way, something must also be materially based in the properly consciousness-producing way. (Searle 1982 and 1984 argues this position.) This philosophical controversy is taken up in the second part of the book: Given a nuts-and-bolts, computer-chip robot that passes any reasonable behavioral test you throw at it, are there any possible grounds on which to maintain that although it seems to be conscious, nevertheless it is not really conscious?

I will argue that there *might* be such grounds. That is, we can *imagine* grounds that would warrant the conclusion that some device, although it passed all the behavioral tests, nevertheless was not conscious. I will also argue that this position has not been properly justified to date. Critics of this view have been correct in objecting that no principle or even type of principle has been supplied to illustrate the possibility of a contrast between 'any old embodiment of some rational agency program' and 'an embodiment in a material system that has the causal powers to produce consciousness'. The account presented here attempts to provide such a principle. However, the principle appealed to, functional preemption, would seem to be so improbable a feature to be found actually embodied in the human brain that the argument is primarily one of conceptual interest and, thus, provides only cold comfort to the Searlian.

Accordingly, we must be prepared to consider the consequences for consciousness ascriptions if our brains are discovered to contain no functional preemption — that is, if our brains are mechanical systems in which physics is always in the service of function or at least never preempted by it. On the assumption that human brains are machines, we would not have the grounds to withhold the ascription of consciousness to the mechanical humanoid android of our construction. But what of the very primitive rational agents, the primitive language-learning, language-using androids such as those, I claim in Part 1, we are already in a position to build? Are they or would they be properly described as conscious agents? In short, the assumption that the brain is a machine gives rise to the question of degrees of consciousness.

In the penultimate section of Part 2, I consider emotional life, sophistication of concepts learnable, breadth of attention and memory spans, and development of a recognizable ego structure as factors to take into account in the ascription of degrees of consciousness, on the assumption that no odd causal arrangement such as functional preemption is found to obtain in the human case. When these factors of consciousness are entered into the picture, it is possible to present a complete procedure for answering our question as to whether a device of the sort contemplated in Part 1 would really be conscious. This procedure is summarized in the final section of Part 2.

Having seen the direction in which the AI research continuum toward a conscious machine lies, and having a procedure in place for assessing ascription of consciousness to devices at various points along the continuum, we still have to ask, especially if we have confirmed that the human brain is indeed mechanistic, "*How* can a machine be conscious?" And the old determinism and choice issues would also be revived with sharp empirical force. In Part 3, I offer a Mystic's response to these questions. The reader is hereby warned that Part 3 is a dessert that may appeal only to people with rather catholic philosophical tastes.

PART ONE

The Engineer's Project

1

Interagency Attribution and Android Skepticism

There are currently a number of overlapping reasons for skepticism about the likelihood of our ever facing 'the android problem' — that is, of our ever building a robot that appears to be conscious on all behavioral tests.

A deep source of skepticism is what has been called 'the frame issue'. For a robot to function in a complex environment, it must be able to switch frames of references to accommodate the sorts of tacit and common-sense knowledge that saturates our experience, our interpretation of it, and our response to it. At the moment we are very much in the dark about the very nature of the problem. We don't know how to represent it in terms precise enough that we can begin to strategize solutions to it. The skeptic concludes, then, that human cognition is not amenable to computational modelling (Dreyfus 1979).

The cognitive science version of the same problem has to do with the elusiveness and apparent generality of the central processing mechanisms of the brain. Although there are aspects of brain functioning that are specific and modular, and hence amenable even at this early stage to various primitive hypotheses concerning the computational structures they might embody, the learning and representation accomplished overall seem so diffuse and general as to be impenetrable to specific hypotheses. There is considerable controversy between centralists and modularists at present; but until modularists come up with hypotheses concerning the specific means whereby modules are integrated, both skeptics and centralists will conclude that there is as yet no proper foundation for the computational hope (Gardner 1985, pp. 130-137).

The philosopher's basis of skepticism has to do with the nature of rationality, intentionality, and linguistic behavior. We do not have grounds to regard an entity as using language, or even as appearing to use language, unless it meets certain conditions. The sorts of conditions the linguistic philosopher might have in mind were first brought to wide philosophical attention by Grice in a context having little — indeed, nothing explicitly — to do with the issues of mind and mechanism (Grice 1957). His analysis of 'non-natural meaning', however, can provide us with a useful application. The view of non-natural meaning as requiring that the audience and the communicator recognize the communicator's intention that the audience take something to be a vehicle of an act of communication can provide one with a test for an apparently language-using entity's properly being so described. In *Rationality* (1964), Jonathan Bennett describes various tests for communication genuineness and develops the notion that essential to something's being a rational agent is its capacity to make dated and universal judgments. His analysis of the way we might test for genuineness of these sorts of judgments is of direct relevance for the inspection of putatively intelligent and rational AI devices, and it includes elements of the Gricean conditions (p. 47) as well as various extensions of it. Accordingly, in citing the features of language on which one focuses when attempting to test for the capacity of some device to embody the Gricean feature of language and Bennett's criterion for rationality, I shall refer to the Grice-Bennett presuppositions of language use and rationality. As we shall shortly see, these features may be characterized as the 'basic interagency attributive features' of language use and rationality.

In brief, the idea is as follows: Suppose we make a space journey and land on some planet. On this planet there are things that move about, and we begin to wonder if they might be advanced intelligences. They seem benign enough in their dealings with us, so we try to teach them our language. We show one a stone, and say 'stone', and so on. But to be able to have accomplished even this much, we have to assume that when we showed the creature a stone, the creature was looking at the stone, or somehow had the stone in its perceptual attention. Thus to be able to engage a putative intelligence in conversation, or to try to, involves the identification of its perceptual organs or medium and the exterior signs of the operations of that medium which enable us to judge that it has been attending to something. Hence the attribution of perception is a prerequisite of the basic sort of testing we do. To test for referential language and purposive agency (as opposed to the mere mirroring or transformation of mathematical pulses of various kinds) requires both independent attribution of perceptual attention and independent attribution of movement as issuing from a specific intention. ("The sound produced was deliberately produced.") Based on such elementary interagency attributions, and based only on such, can the complex reciprocal interagency attributions such as are embodied in the Gricean condition be made.

But now if we try to apply these attributions to artificial devices that take input from a keyboard and give output in the form of roman characters on a monitor, we are stymied. There is no *spread* between perception and conception. So the Turing test (which states, roughly, that when we can't discriminate between a human's effort to deceive and a computer's responses, both given to us via a monitor output, we've got a thinking computer) doesn't even enable us to make the very tests we want. No skeptic will be convinced by a set-up that forbids our making the most immediate and natural sorts of tests we would put to an extraterrestrial creature (Turing 1963). (For related criticisms of the Turing test, see Gunderson 1971, Chapter 2.)

More generally, the philosopher will hold that a device should not be described as being a rational agent, or a being capable of using language, unless there are specific grounds for attributing to the device the understanding (or apparent understanding, since the illusion is all we are interested in at this stage) that it *is* a rational agent, or that it is using language. It should be possible to test the device for its 'knowledge' of whether the linguistic output it is presenting is being received by some other entity or not. It should discriminate between situations when it is, as it takes it, in the presence of no other agent, and when it is in the presence of some other agent. It should have criteria of belief attribution to other agents independent of language. To date, no human-to-artificial-agent interactive program has been created to embody or successfully meet even the most minimal aspect of the Grice-Bennett presuppositions of language use and rationality. Without a discussion of such a program, it is unclear whether AI theorists' contemplation of a robot that genuinely uses language is a pipe dream or not.

Finally, there is the skepticism arising from what is essentially a consequence of our inadequate understanding of the frame problem and of the nature of central processing in cognition: Although a wide variety of expert systems has been created, little investigation has been done on the ways in which these various programs might be integrated into coherent, putatively personal systems. The categories of the individual areas are well agreed upon and have been much discussed in relative isolation from each other. Among these categories are perception, pattern recognition, motivation, abduction, planning, retrieval, attention, executive or motor, knowledge representation, linguistic representation, and learning. But few indeed have been the efforts to discuss the ways in which these might be associated with each other. One attempt in the general direction of such a project is the Dennett article mentioned earlier, "Towards a Cognitive Theory of Consciousness" (1978a). Dennett is the first to admit the deficiencies of his flowchart effort. For example, he says of his control representation that "the control component in my model is awfully fancy . . . It has a superb capacity to address just the right stored information in its long term memory, a talent for asking M just the right questions, and an ability to organize its long and short term goals and plans in a very versatile way. This is no homunculus that any AI researcher has the faintest idea how to realize at this time" (p. 164). He also anticipates objections to it of the form, "Such an entity would not even *seem* to have an inner conscious life because . . . it lacks any provision for such human phenomena as . . . it ignores . . ." (p. 172).

Let's consider now in what way Dennett's flowchart accommodates or fails to accommodate the problems mentioned. The frame problem is mentioned, as we've just seen, but not discussed. The worries stand. Similarly, the central processing problems are covered, so to speak, under the 'problem solving' rubric, but no details are available of course. And, finally, the area whereby the Grice-Bennett presuppositions of language use would be met is not in any way called to our attention. Indeed, it's not clear at first glance whether the flowchart accommodates, in the barest sense of allowing room for, the details that would embody the processes that meet Grice-Bennett presuppositions. On closer inspection it appears that there *is* room, provided we allow some basic rethinking, as I hope will be clear to the reader who wishes to check again after completing Part 1 of the book. But without further discussion the skeptic will remain unconvinced about the practicability of something that meets Grice-Bennett test presuppositions.

Similarly, whatever the problem-solving unit is geared to accomplish, it should be able to include the ability to learn a second language, not to mention the ability to learn a first language. A first-language-acquisition means of some sort (even if it is an application of more general strategies) is a vital component of any putatively conscious robot. But without a discussion of some of the details of such a component, the skeptic will feel justified in regarding the task of creating the illusion of a personal consciousness as impenetrable. And the Dennett flowchart no more (and no less, to be fair) accommodates a language-acquisition device than it does the means whereby a device might meet the Grice-Bennett presuppositions of language use and rationality.

I will now suggest that any device capable of meeting Gricean conditions of non-natural meaning or Bennett's conditions of genuine language use and rationality must have the ability to perform 'basic interagency attributions'. We may say that a device which can perform basic interagency attributions has a basic interagency program. The task of determining the likelihood of there ever being a device that meets Grice-Bennett behavioral presuppositions by performing basic interagency attributions is accomplished by an assessment of the feasibility of constructing a basic interagency attribution program. We then turn to the demands of such an enterprise — a rather lengthy business, as it turns out. And this is followed by a discussion of the implications of such a program for the other grounds of skepticism.

The features of Grice's account of the contrast between natural and non-natural meaning that are of relevance to us are simple to state. When one performs some activity as a vehicle of communicating with someone else, one intends that the audience receive the message; one also intends that the audience be aware of one's intention that the audience receive the message. And this awareness or recognition of the audience will itself be part of the audience's reasons for accepting the message in the way intended by the one who produced it. The implications of this point for the aspect of semantic theory that is not subsumed within cognitive science need not concern us. To be sure, it was not for cognitive science that Grice presented his analysis of this feature of non-natural meaning. But its usefulness in AI design does not depend upon its success in its original context. Similarly, and at the risk of redundancy, Bennett's tests have the aim of illuminating the nature of rationality and language use. His is the philosopher's task of presenting a general account or theory of the topic. Our application does not depend on that account. Indeed Bennett (1976) has substantially revised the account of *Rationality*, but the grounds for the revision do not affect our rather elementary use of his analysis of the intentionality of rationality. Also, it is interesting to note that Grice's work in philosophical psychology does not apply his insights in semantic theory. In "Method in Philosophical Psychology" (1975), Grice elaborates some aspects of creature design which ensure that the creatures have independent survival-related purposes. But Grice falls short of considering those competences that enable a creature to satisfy the Gricean analysis of non-natural meaning.

We proceed, then, under the assumption that people will be using these tests on an AI device: Consciously or subconsciously, they will be attempting to apply interagency attribution tests. Basic interagency attributions comprise the following:

1. Agentive presence: "That is an agent."
2. Agent's focus of attention: "That agent is looking there."
3. Belief: "That agent believes there is food in the room."

    4. Desire: "That agent is hungry."
    5. Plan: "That agent plans to kick the ball."
    6. Agent's movement: "That agent moved its limb."

Over and above these basic interagency attributions are attributions of all and sundry mental states: "That agent is afraid of ants," or "That agent is choosing between the apples and the oranges," or "That agent is communicating a message to me."

Implicit in this presentation of the basic interagency attributions is a theory that agentive presence, attentive focus, belief, desire, plan, and agent movement issuing from intention constitute a complete set, and that all particular interagency attributions can be represented as the combinations of content-filled basic interagency attributions. I will not attempt to support this theory at this stage. Instead, I will be working under the hypothesis that unless these six forms of interagency attribution can be performed by some device, it will not be capable of meeting the interagency attribution requirements of rationality and language use.

We will now look at the relationship between the concept of intentionality and intentional system meant in the most general sense and the specific intentionality of interagency attribution. In its most general sense, the concept of intentionality concerns the taking by some system of some entity as an object. The problem is that we do not have any inclination to regard a television camera pointed at a table as a system that takes the table to be an object. If we do, then any transaction appears to have intentionality and the concept has faded into contrastlessness. For there to be a difference between systems that are intentional and systems that are not, we need to have an idea of the conditions such systems meet that the other systems do not. This requirement leads the AI artist down many theoretical blind alleys: We begin to wonder immediately whether the consciousness that would provide the difference can possibly have any conditions or marks, and so on.

We may stay more on track by observing that if there is to be a contrast between intentional systems and nonintentional systems, it will be a contrast that is *used* by an intentional system. Moreover, an intentional system will apply the concept to itself. An intentional system has the capacity to take itself to take things for objects. And it has the capacity to hypothesize of other entities that they are taking things to be objects. Thus, I am an intentional system, and I take it that some of the objects I take as objects are themselves intentional systems. But on what basis may I do this? I observe that there are to begin with these three basic modalities in which objects are given to me: Objects are given to me through perception, thought, and desire. Another way to put it is to say that I am given three basic types of objects: spatiotemporal objects, conceptual objects, and desires. Through composition I end up with 'plan' or 'intended movement'. Or, to put it differently, through composition I end up with the notion of 'agent', a system in which perception, thought, desire, and (through composition) movement are coordinated around the satisfaction of desire. Finally, then, I have a way of attributing intentionality. I attribute intentionality to something that exhibits agency. But agency is itself something I must attribute to an object. On what basis may I do that?

I can look for evidence of perception, desire, and belief in the behavior of a system. The integrating concept here is 'desire'. And to look for evidence of perception, desire, and belief requires filling in a behavior pattern blank, so to speak:

/A desires D, & (A perceives P so) A believes B/
so move(s) M occur(s)

Now, any moves or occurrences can be interpreted by using a pattern such as this one: There is no move whatever that *cannot* be interpreted with reference to an attribution of this kind. The ancient view that "the world is full of gods" is precisely an attribution of this kind — as is the view that all things happen through Providence. I do not need to take it that I have located the perceptual organ or medium to make this attribution. All I need is a moving body, which I then identify as the body of an agent or the limb of an agent (which identification constitutes the attribution of agentive presence); the rest is attribution and can be as fanciful as I like. If there is any Quinean radical indeterminacy (Quine 1960), it would begin with agentive attribution and infect everything else that requires it, such as language, since communication requires the attribution of speech action, hence of agency. Radical indeterminacy would not begin with language use, much less with translation from one language to another. Conversely, if competing agency attributions of this very basic kind can be sorted out by evidence, then such procedures will 'cure' suspicions of principled indeterminacy by the same means right down the linguistic line. Can such basic competing attributions be sorted out by evidence?

The philosopher, of course, is interested in whether sorting out competing attributions by observation of behavior is justified, and by which principles, if at all. We agency illusionists, however, are interested in a rather different question — namely, by what principles *do* we sort out competing attributions, or establish our attributions, whether these principles are justified or not. Moreover, to be practical, the philosopher needs to get muddied in the latter question in order to analyze the former.

Neglect of this practical matter has led some philosophers into difficulty. Consider, for example, Davidson's views in "Agency" (1980). He there asserts that so long as one's moves can be described under an aspect that makes them intentional, an act has been performed. If by this he means "so long as one's moves are correctly describable as intentional," then he is merely making a request for a theory of rival intentional description, since *all* moves can be described as intentional, and each move can be described as intentional in an indefinite number of ways. If he means that any move that fits a description as an intentional doing *is* the act of an agent, then flowers are agents or the limbs of agents. If he means to restrict his analysis of agency to contexts in which the attribution of agentive presence has securely been established, then his analysis can't help but be empty, as the discrimination between an agent's doings and an agent's nondoings will surely depend on the very means used to discriminate an agent's doings from mere nondoings — that is, on the means by which we securely or properly establish agentive presence. To put this another way, he has missed the opportunity to address the heart of the motivating question. How do we distinguish the doings of an agent from mere happenings? How do we establish agentive presence, given that each event can be supplied with indefinitely many agentive stories?

How then do we properly discriminate between rival accounts of the same set of moves? We take our cue from how people do make agentive presence attributions or, to put it another way, from a cognitive scientist's model of our competence in making such attributions. The notion of competence here does not entail propriety but merely specific procedures. If the philosopher is to have an account of propriety, it will come in the form of an assessment of the procedures we use from the standpoint of the metaphysician. The ontological presuppositions of our procedures will be evaluated. Our job here, however, is to use such procedures in understanding not only what behavior a system must evidence for us to take it to be an agent, and hence for us to take it to be intentional, but also what structures a system must contain for it to be able to make similar discriminations regarding the moves it perceives as events in its environment.

The first element to draw out is the expansion of the action or behavior pattern mentioned above so as to include a specific plan. Thus:

/A desires D, & (A perceives P, so) A believes B/
so A plans PL so/ move(s) M occur(s)

The inclusion of a plan enables rival accounts to be assessed, since some of the plan attributions will continue to make sense and some won't as the behavior of the system being studied is monitored. We may, for example, suspect or hold to indeterminacy between two rival desire attributions in a situation in which a system is relating to some objects in a patterned way. Say every so often a body is seen to move toward a second body. It then makes contact with it and behaves in a distinct way; for example, it shivers. We may take it that the shiver is a sign of distress; we may take it that the shiver is a sign of satisfaction. Our desire attributions here conflict. But if we notice some part of the body moving in a way functionally related to the orientation of the body to the second body, whereby the motion precedes the motion of the body toward the second body, then we may attribute to it the plan to make contact with the second body. There are still conflicting attributions — for example, the contact gives the body great pleasure that is not manifest in outward behavior measurable by us, and the shiver is a sign of minor distress — but we prefer the account that fills out the pattern with visibles to one that multiplies invisibles, other things being equal.

Second, we look for evidence that a system acts in ways that satisfy its *interests*. The notion of interests, of course, requires appraisal by us. But a root interest, if not the root interest, is survival. Further, survival is an objectively determinable interest. And so a fundamental procedure is to check behavior to see if it is founded on survival-gaining patterns.

By these two means I may attribute the holding of independent purposes to some system. But I will withhold the attribution of intentionality and of rational agency until I have grounds for attributing to the system the attribution of agency to others. This, then, is the third main element of these procedures, the attribution of agency to a system that is judged to be an agency-attributive system. This attribution, however, appears to be epistemologically vicious. To resolve this paradox is to cut the Gordian knot of agency attribution: We break the epistemological circle by attempting to engage the creature in conversation. I judge that something attributes agency to others by seeing whether it will attribute agency to me, and I judge that it attributes agency to me when I can teach it my language, or learn its language, and engage it in conversation, and interact with it linguistically, and extralinguistically, in the interagency manner — that is, to the satisfaction of our respective independent purposes and, perhaps, to the satisfaction of the other's purposes as well.

Whether the structured behavior and underlying representational structure of an interagentive system fully exhausts its intentionality is of course the deep philosophical problem of consciousness. But so long as we are concerned merely with the appearance or illusion of intentionality, interagency attribution and the structure of independent purposes are at the decisive center of such an appearance. If scientists want to make something that appears to be conscious, they could do no better than to start by making something whose behavior exhibits the structure of the holding of independent purposes as well as the structure of interagency attributions within which, and only within which, language learning, language use, and rationality can take place and be tested for.

Among the existing programs, some of the 'vehicles' of Valentino Braitenberg would exhibit independent purposes (Braitenberg 1984) but not interagency attribution. On the other hand, the work in multi-agent planning currently going on (Brown 1980; Bruce and Newman 1978; Salveter 1979; Ringle 1982; Hobbs and Evans 1980; etc.) provides some of the groundwork at different levels for interagency attribution but is neither perception-based nor joined to independent purpose holding systems in imaginary-real environments (as with Braitenberg's vehicles) or microworld environments with which humans can interact or into which humans can enter using microworld or representative bodies. It is also noteworthy that works such as Johnson-Laird (1983), Minsky (1986), and Jackendoff (1987), though so thorough in other respects, fail to treat the problems of interagency attribution altogether.

I will call an artificial device whose behavior captures the structure of basic interagency attribution (including, for terminological convenience, the holding of independent purposes) and whose underlying representational structures embody such behavior or are the means whereby its behavior comes to be so structured, a device which has 'a basic interagency program'. Our question now is, Can a basic interagency program be built? We may assume either that any device with an interagency program will appear to be conscious, or that no device which does not have an interagency program is likely to appear to be conscious. The strategy provided here is justifiable either way. My claim in Part 1 of the book is that we already have the ability to build a device with a basic interagency program.

To put this another way, theories *like* Jonathan Bennett's theory of rationality — "the expression of dated and universal judgements is both necessary and sufficient for rationality" (Bennett 1964, p. 94) — may or may not be correct. But the kinds of tests they presuppose are persuasively relevant to the AI artists. Indeed, they presuppose a whole range of interagency tests, including the requirement that there be a spread (as I've put it) between perception, conception, and motor functioning, as well as between distinct types of conception (Bennett 1964, pp. 42, 47, 88, 90). These tests are relevant in several ways. To the degree that they may be presupposed by more than one theory, the tests may be correct without some particular theory being quite the right theory. Second, of course, some such theory may be the right theory and therefore the tests are the right tests. Third, and most important, sophisticated observers will be using these tests because they believe the theories; and less sophisticated observers too may use the tests, consciously or subconsciously, because, rightly or wrongly, they operate under the assumptions of some of the theories that presuppose the tests.

To put all of this negatively, there is a rich source of skepticism here that must be addressed. To put it positively, basic interagency attribution is a competence that implies a study whose job it is to specify the computational formalisms, if any such are specifiable, whereby such attributions may be performed. Armed with such accounts, the agency illusionists have their work cut out for them. Competence models of processes of interagency attribution are the mirrors with which such illusionary equipment can be built.

2

Pure Versus Impure Models
of Agency

Our considerations now must be strategic rather than even loosely philosophical. The principal instrument of strategy for human-to-machine interactive interagency attributive programming, I suggest, is the distinction between perception-based and non-perception-based models of agent functioning. We may approach this distinction with a look at the range of existing programs.

For our purposes, we may classify existing programs in the following way:

1. Android-leading robotics programs
2. Microworld environments with agents
3. Cognitive subsystem models
4. Useful or entertaining expert systems

The first category is meant to include robot-skiers, robot-pianists, artificial limbs, and various sophisticated robotic tools used in manufacture. What distinguishes this category from the other two is that in this group the stress is not on 'internal cognition' but on motor performances (Minsky, ed., 1985). There is a healthy optimism in the field of robotics, and even Hubert Dreyfus recognizes the legitimacy of the aspirations of robotics work (Dreyfus & Dreyfus 1986, p. xiii).

However, optimism about robotic limbs, aids to the handicapped, and assembly-line workers does not translate into grounds for optimism about the cognitive component that would also be necessary, obviously, for the construction of a machine that gives the appearance of being a conscious creature.

Presumably, the fact that our limbs and muscles can be mechanically simulated is not the primary controversy here. Moreover, since someone whose motor capacity is restricted to the type of movement already simulable by an artificial arm or grasper or a series of such may still be a full-fledged rational agent, our ability to eventually simulate all the complex functioning of human motor devices is not germane to the heart of the issue, the burden of which falls on our ability to model the functioning of rational agency in general and human agency in particular along mechanical lines. Accordingly, the challenge we are setting for ourselves is to see whether we might take a robot arm mounted on motorized wheels of some sort and attach it to a program that receives information about the environment in a primary sensory mode (presumably visual, tactile, or auditory) and, to a program that operates upon this information so as to yield motor output, the implementation of which exhibits the structure of rational agency.

Since the greatest part of the burden falls on the cognitive calculation program, the entire undertaking can be implemented in a purely formal system. We save ourselves the expense of building the robot-arm by representing its functioning formally; likewise, we don't need to use an actual television camera but, instead, can represent the analysis of visual information in formal terms. And, finally, we can take these formal analyses and represent the functioning of the agent in its microworld to humans watching the program work on a monitor. This has been called 'microworld programming'.

We are brought, thus, to our second category of program: formal models of agent functioning visually represented to us in some video format. An early but obscure example of such a program (which I have chosen for a reason that will become clear shortly) is Walter Jacob's PERCY, described in Jacob's "How a Bug's Mind Works" (Jacobs 1972). PERCY is a nest-builder and -eater. Its environment contains a variety of objects, some of which constitute PERCY's food and some of which are the stuff out of which the nest is to be built. A wall divides the environment into distinct areas, and there are landmarks with reference to which PERCY can orient positions. PERCY's body has an arm and a sense organ, or eye, oriented in a certain direction and with an angle of vision.

In order for a program to be a represented formal model of agent functioning, there will have to be a unit of the program that represents the agent, a subsystem of which will represent the sensory functioning of the agent, a subsystem of which will represent the motor functioning of the agent, and the mediating subsystem of which will represent the cognitive functioning or calculation that receives the sensory representations and through whose operations instructions are finally given to the motor subsystem. In addition there will have to be a unit that represents the environment and also rules the conditions whereby one environmental state changes into another. And of course there will have to be another level of representation altogether whereby the formal elements receive a visual interpretation so that they can be witnessed by us on a video monitor.

I will say that a represented formal model of an agent is 'pure' when all new information received by the cognition is given through the sensory channel or channels. I've chosen PERCY because it is one of the few pure agent models described in the literature. All of PERCY's information about food location, nest location, and so on is given by what it is represented as seeing.

By contrast, Terry Winograd's SHRDLU (Winograd 1972) is an 'impure' represented formal model of agency functioning. SHRDLU represents an agent that is a mobile robot arm in a room with cubes, blocks, and pyramids of various colors on a table or on the floor. SHRDLU has a perceptual organ that can see these objects, discriminating one from another, and an interpretive system that can represent the configuration of blocks and pyramids it sees. SHRDLU also has sensory-motor coordination, which enables it to manipulate, lift, and transport the pyramids and blocks according to its instructions. SHRDLU is a visually represented formal model of agency functioning, rather than an android leading robotics program, because the hardware has not been constructed. There is no robot arm, no table with cubes and pyramids, and no camera. There is only the representation of such things on a screen and the underlying formal representations with which the computer operates.

SHRDLU is an *impure* represented formal model of agency because, in addition to the sensory information its camera eye gleans, it receives input in the form of English sentences coming directly from the human operating the program. And, in addition to the instructions to the motor unit, the mobile arm, and the camera, SHRDLU generates output directly in the form of English sentences. Thus SHRDLU has two forms of input: information coming from its sense organ about the environment and input in the form of English assertions, questions, and commands. And it has two forms of output: motor behavior involving the motion of the camera and the grasper and output in the form of assertions and questions in English.

SHRDLU can perform a wide variety of task instructions. It can respond to instructions to grasp the largest red cube and move it to the right of the smallest blue pyramid, for instance. It will question an instruction it doesn't understand. It will interpret statements from the operator assigning proper names to various items in the environment and subsequently respond appropriately to instructions using the new proper names. It will initiate intermediate steps required to fulfill some task instruction. It will appropriately answer questions about why it has done certain things, distinguishing between the things it has done in order to be able to do what was asked of it and the things it has done because it was asked or instructed to do them by the operator. It will appropriately answer questions about the locations of various items in the environment.

But SHRDLU is an impure model of agency functioning because it receives information in unmediated cognitive form, rather than exclusively through its sensory channel. It has no way of distinguishing between elements in its environment that are linguistic acts or symbols and those that are not. It has no way of conceiving that an agent which produces language can be part of an environment. Similarly, it has no way of conceiving that some of its motor activity might be in the service of communication with an agent that is part of some large-scale environment. If there were some problems with its direct linguistic output channel, it could never substitute making symbols with its robot arm — nor could it be taught to do so. Its language was never learned and never could be learned. In order for language to be learnable, there has to be a phase in which certain things in the environment come to be conceptualized as linguistic symbols. Information coming in through the sensory channel or channels becomes conceptualized or represented as linguistic, and all use of language is rooted in and seen as rooted in sensory and motor exchanges with the environment.

Winograd's interest in constructing SHRDLU was in the modelling of the understanding of a natural language. The model world was constructed to give an extension, even if only a formal one, to the semantic concepts. It was not necessary for his purposes to model the functioning of agency in an entirely pure way. In this sense, the focus of the research in SHRDLU is not the modelling of agency qua agency but the modelling of some subsystem of agency.

SHRDLU thus belongs as much in our third category of program, the modelling of various cognitive subsystems, as in our second category, the modelling of the functioning of an agent in an environment. And it is within this third category, of course, that a vast proliferation of work has occurred in the last fifteen or twenty years. The main areas of work relevant to this inquiry have been in pattern recognition, knowledge representation, retrieval systems, learning systems, linguistic representation, and the modelling of the fundamental procedures of cognition using schema systems, production systems, and connectionist or parallel processing models. (For an overview see Anderson 1984.)

Cognitive and computer scientists in each of these areas have been

ALLEGHENY COLLEGE LIBRARY

testing the reaches of particular approaches to particular problems in cognitive modelling. So the critic of AI ambitions would be right to say that the knowledge we have gained through the modelling of cognitive subsystems has not been applied yet to the global problems of modelling rational agency. But such a critic would not be right to imply that insuperable obstacles have been found which prevent the elaboration of a pure model of agency to the degree that it becomes the model of a rational agent surviving in an environment and capable of learning the rudiments of a natural language, such as English, from a human instructor represented to it as an element in its environment.

A deepening understanding of human cognitive processes and the possible structures of cognition in any intentional system depends upon ever more sophisticated cognitive subsystem programs. There is also the hope of an eventual integration of perceptual, epistemic, motivational, abductive, retrieval, motor, and linguistic systems at an extremely sophisticated level. But the key to the demonstration of the feasibility, plausibility, and eminently practical nature of this enterprise lies in the construction of pure models of rational agents that are adapted to environments rigorously simplified to allow for the stringing together of elementary perceptual, epistemic, motivational, abductive, retrieval, motor, and linguistic systems in a properly integrated way. The key to demonstrating the feasibility of interagency programming is maintaining the purity of the program. Once we attend to the demands of purity in microworld interagency programming, we can see the path that must be taken. The restriction of purity itself provides a demand that guides us toward a properly structured theory.

Accordingly, we set ourselves the following task: We are attempting to determine whether and to what degree it is possible (assuming it is possible to some degree) to program a device, a model agent (Agent-1), that operates in a microworld. One element of this microworld is the 'body' of another agent operated by a human (Agent-2), to whom the microworld is represented on a monitor, such that an untutored or relatively untutored human, after a period of observing how the model agent (Agent-1) survives and otherwise performs in its environment, will be able to teach Agent-1 a range of basic words of the human's natural language (whatever that may be) via operations of the model agent-body (Agent-2). These operations will be represented or given to Agent-1 as environmental elements only and will therefore be received by Agent-1 through its model perception only. Naturally, we are interested not only in the degree to that humans would be able to teach Agent-1 words for use in elementary language games such as 'where's such-and-such?' but also in the degree to which conversations serving

Agent-1's survival and other (e.g., danger-avoidance) purposes might be had by Agent-1 with the human via Agent-2, and in the degree of open-endedness and creativity such conversations might take. In short, our task in what follows is guided by the demands of designing a system that will create the appearance of agency.

3

Integrated System Programming

The system we have in mind, then, will consist of the following elements:

1. Model environment: This includes a model ontology, as well as a model physics, which provides a successor state for each environmental state.
2. Model Agent-1: This is one of the objects of the environment and its program, which is the central focus of our investigation.
3. Model Agent-2: This appears in the environment as an object, but its doings are controlled by a human.
4. Input Device: This is the device with which the human operator of Agent-2 operates Agent-2.
5. Transaction Program: This is the program whereby the system organizes instructions from Agent-1, instructions from the Input Device, and the current environmental state so that the model physical program can calculate the successor state and implement it.
6. Monitors: Several monitors show different aspects of the environment. One shows the whole environment. One shows Agent-1's 'viewpoint'. One shows Agent-2's 'viewpoint'.
7. Representation Program: This is the program whereby each state of the environment is represented to us on the monitors.

In order to create the appearance of Agent-1's having independent purposes, we will build its program up by following the general lines of evolution. We may also think of ourselves as elaborating the environment as required in order for the various capacities of Agent-1 to match a world and be exercised in a world sufficiently complex that these capacities may be seen to be adaptive.

Following this approach, the main elements of Agent-1's program are as follows:

1. Model Hunger and Food Search
2. Danger Avoidance and Pain Behavior
3. Mapmaking and Map Use
4. Causal Analysis

These four elements are intended to create the appearance of Agent-1's having independent purposes. The elements with which we approach interagency attribution are:

5. Analysis of the Actions of a Second Agent
6. Acquiring a Natural Language Lexicon
6. Purposive Use of The Acquired Terms

Model Ontology

The essential ingredients of a model ontology as required for a *pure* human-to-machine interactive interagency attributive program are a set of objects, a set of features these objects may have, and a set of locations. We may begin with the blocks world described by Terry Winograd in *Understanding Natural Language* (Winograd 1972, Chapter 7). Alternatively, we may think of the environment as organized into n locations, and of the objects of this world as occupying one and only one location each. But each object may be in a number of states according to the presence or absence of various features. Either way, the representation program will transform the model entities into familiar icons for viewing by humans on the monitor. We will elaborate the details of the model ontology as required to match or provide a context for the target abilities of Agent-1.

Model Physics and Transaction Program

In most of what follows we will not call explicit attention to the demands of these two programs. We will assume, rather, that such programs will carry on the functions required to ensure that the inputs from Agent-1 to the System, the inputs from the Input Device to the System, and the previous state of the environment as a whole considered as an input to the System will result in a single overall successor state. For example, if in one state Agent-1 shows its locomotor engaged toward direction D, and the next location in direction D from Agent-1 is empty, then in the successor state Agent-1 will appear in the next location, so long as Agent-2 wasn't heading for that location as well, and so long as no other object was moving into that location, and so on. In the case of competing instructions, the Transaction Program might either arbitrarily assign victors or assign victors by temporally prioriz-ing the inputs.

Surviving

Model Hunger and Food Search

For something to have the appearance of being a purposive system, it will have to be identifiable as a unit. Our representation program will provide a familiar icon of an agent: First, there will be something that looks like a limb or grasper, something that looks like a locomotor, something whose movements and shape suggest that it might be an organ of perception, something like a mouth from which model sounds will issue, and a trunk that unifies these parts.

Second, its behavior will have to appear to be governed by some principle or other. In particular, it will have to appear as though its perception enables it to pick out elements of its environment that are specifically related to the implementation of that principle. To fulfill this requirement, it will appear to be avoiding some of the elements of its environment and/or to be seeking out other elements of its environ-ment. Indeed, the assumption of an observer that something is an organ of perception is justified by the relation that the movements and positions of the possible organ of perception have to the subsequent motions of parts of the structure that one is examining to see whether or not it might be a purposive system.

It is tempting to hold that we might be able to make hypotheses of some system to the effect that it is a purposive system without its having to have any organ of perception. Why, for instance, can't we see a medical diagnosis expert system as being a purposive system that has as its goal the answering of questions that are put to it? The trouble is that in such a situation we have one thing that is undeniably an agent — the human user — and something else that might or might not be a purposive system *on its own*. In order to rule out the possibility that the medical diagnostic system is a mere tool of human agency, a mere artificial cognitive limb, so to speak, that is successively attached to each human user who puts a question to the system, the observer will want to see if it has any purposes *on its own* apart from any interagency context.

But for something to have purposes apart from an interagency context, these purposes will have to be manifested by its behavior. Since the behavior of more or less anything can be seen to be principle-governed, anything will be a candidate for a purposive system, and we will need something over and above the mere fact of principle-governed behavior to constitute the evidence of purpose. Thus we want to be led from the fact of principle-governed behavior to a much richer sort of attribution — namely, that the principle which governs the behavior of some system serves the *interests* of the system. The attribution of purpose, then, is dependent on the attribution of interests.

The most fundamental interest something can have is its own survival. The fulfillment of any other interest through some behavior involves some duration; and if the system cannot expect to survive even that period, it cannot expect to fulfill any interest at all. Of course, there is a complex relationship between something's being motivated by something other than survival (e.g., pleasure) and its achievement of its survival by doing the things that give it pleasure (e.g., eating). But from the strategic point of view, it's safe to say that a system which appears to secure its own survival will have as good a chance as any to appear to be a system with an independent purpose. We can say of some system that it is experiencing pleasure only by recognizing the specific marks or forms of expressing pleasure that it has. And we will not judge that a system has any true experiences, or that any behavior is expressive of an experience, until we have independent reason to regard it as an intentional system. The attribution of interests other than survival such as pleasure, then, will be made only after both tests of independent purposes and tests of the capacity to function in the interagency manner have been passed. Thus, although we conceive of pleasure as a basic interest, we will not identify something as having this interest before we have identified it as something that is capable of being described as having interests. And to identify it in the latter way, then, requires that something be identified as an interest in an experience-neutral way. Survival and only survival, apparently, is an interest that works this way. Whether something acts to secure its own survival can be assessed objectively without the attribution of experience or full intentionality.

Thus we begin by modelling a system that behaves in such a way as to secure its own survival. For something to be seen to be securing its own survival, it will have to be seen to be checking for threats to its survival and avoiding them. And for something to be seen to be a threat to its survival, a genuine threat must be set up.

Accordingly, we will model the process of getting hungry, finding food, eating, and receiving nutrition. Our agent will have a perceptual apparatus that, within a certain range and orientation, will discriminate between objects of a certain type, which we'll call 'F' for food, and other objects. The agent has the motor capacity to reorient its body in preparation for locomotion, to move from one location to an adjacent location in the direction of its orientation, and to ingest objects of an appropriate size adjacent to it on some orientation. The agent also has a body clock that measures the time elapsed since it has last ingested objects of type F. When this period of time is sufficiently long, the agent will be in the state of hunger.

The activity of the agent, then, will be to do nothing until it is in the state of hunger, at that point it will locomote until it spots food, at that point it will ingest some food; then it will return to its glorious quiescence until it once again becomes hungry.

In order to ensure that the hunger is based on a model reality, we will provide that the body program of the agent (a part of the model physics) includes the instruction to permanently shut down the function of the agent, erase all its memories, and so on, if the period elapsed since its last ingestion of food exceeds the hunger trigger by a sufficient duration. If the agent is hungry for too long, it 'dies'.

Although we can conceive of a system that has no independent purpose other than its own survival, we are much more naturally inclined to suppose of any intentional system that it has independent purposes or some independent purpose other than its own survival. Imagine an interagency system whose only independent purpose was its own survival. Then, assuming that the capacities it attributes to other agents mirror the attributes it gives itself, its interagency life will be based on the assumption that its own survival and the survival of the other agent are the only purposes to be fulfilled. Such a creature is not likely to appear to be conscious since it does nothing to mark the attribution of conscious experiences to other agents. Thus, the appearance of consciousness in a system pretty much requires the appearance of having experiences and preferences independent of interagency attribution. The modelling of independent purposes thus requires more than the modelling of survival behavior and survival attribution.

In addition to survival through eating, then, we will model marks of satisfaction and distress. Our agent will have three modes of behavior that we call *smile*, *frown*, and *neutral*. At this stage these modes are conditions assumed by the agent depending on how recently it has consumed food. The representation program will present the human observers of the agent with suitably recognizable icons (such as a vocalizer in the shape of a mouth that smiles, frowns, and is neutral.)

Later these conditions will have an important role to play in interagency attribution processes.

Danger Avoidance and Pain Behavior

In addition to survival through eating, the distress of hunger, and its satisfaction, we may give our agent the ability to recognize danger and flee it. Objects in the environment, then, will be classified as F (food) or D (danger). As no potential conflict exists between eating and surviving in the system thus far set up, there is no basis on which the making of significant choices independent of interagency functioning could be attributed to the agent prior to the addition of model danger. But with both hunger-satisfying purposes and danger-fleeing purposes, there is a basis on which an observer can attribute significant choice-making independent of interagency functioning. And the richer the independent purposive life of a system, the easier it is to create the appearance of genuine interagency functioning and, eventually, of full-fledged intentionality, since the proper range of purposive life will be present within it to be able to serve as a basis for a properly varied set of attributions to make of others.

We may, for instance, provide that danger comes in the form of some predator. Avoiding danger involves finding a safe spot. In the environment, there will be pockets of safety in which Agent-1 may hide and into which the danger will not penetrate. Further, there will be specific consequences of being caught. Perhaps the danger will be a predator that nibbles at the agent. When Agent-1 has been nibbled at by a predator, it will frown and its activities will be impaired. Perhaps it will shriek a bit and have fits of shivering as it subsequently goes about its business. It will continue to have such fits until a sufficient period of time has elapsed. If pain is received during some episode in which there is already pain, then perhaps the pain sentences will be served consecutively rather than concurrently. This outcome will reflect the disadvantages of being doubly or trebly attacked during some period. As with the nutrition program, the outcome will reflect both objective circumstances pertaining to the satisfaction of the objective interest of survival and behavior that, when complemented by other tests, will lend itself to the attribution of an experience.

Mapmaking and Map Use

For realism's sake, it would be appropriate to enable the agent to explore without specifically being hungry or fleeing danger. This propensity would be a positive adaptation since the agent would have a greater chance of survival if it has a full and updated map as opposed to an empty map or an out-of-date one. During Explore, then, Agent-1 records what it detects as it arbitrarily moves along: It mapmakes. Unless we are content to make our agent a hyperactive creature, we should also give it a rest clock so that when it is not hungry and not fleeing danger, it is not always exploring.

Causal Analysis

We'll now give our agent another form of learning capacity. Our environment program will model various causal processes. For example, a certain area of the environment will be the fertile area such that, whenever objects of type S (seeds) appear within the fertile area or are brought into the fertile area by some agent, food will appear there within a short period of time. In order to allow for the transportation of seeds from one place to another, we will give the body and motor programs of our agent the relevant rules for grasping objects of a suitable size such as seeds. Presumably, this will render independently usable some feature of the Ingest program whereby food is grasped as part of the ingestion process. We will expand the perceptual program of the agent so as to allow that seeds are distinguishable from other objects as well.

We'll also provide that the time-coding of the map update function uses larger chunks of time than those used for individual perceptual acts or motor acts. In effect, the agent scans and updates an area giving the entire area as scan-updated a new time-code. We can refer to the contents of a map in a single time-code period as a *mapshot*. Furthermore, while the Explore program is dominant, the agent will scan the same area back and forth. It will thus have accurate information about successive mapshots of the areas it explores. Thus one would expect that it will occasionally have a mapshot at T_n, which includes seed at L_n, and a mapshot of T_{n+1} which in turn includes food at L_n.

Next, we provide that during Rest, our agent will analyze the contents of successive mapshots. We will poetically call such analysis *dreaming*. In order to make possible hypothesis construction concerning causal regularities, we give the agent an empty *cause file* at its birth. Each of its innately perceivable object types will be associated with an initially empty causal slot. Dream analysis will study successive mapshots and prepare hypotheses about causal regularities. These hypotheses will then be stored in memory and retrieved for testing in an active manner while the agent is engaged in its Explore routine. The Explore routine, then, branches (in an arbitrary though weighted way) into

Map-updating and Test causal hypotheses prepared during dreaming.

Causal hypotheses themselves can be quite simple in form: A causal regularity will be a state of affairs within a mapshot that is regularly followed by some other state of affairs within the successive mapshot. Variables as restricted as type of object and location of object would suffice. The causal hypothesis constructor would then search during Rest for sudden change in object type occupying the same location in successive mapshots, after eliminating motion or locomotion as the account of the sudden appearance of the new token of the new object type.

With the analysis of successive mapshots we have begun to lay the groundwork for the development of interagent programming, since the extraction of action sequences from perception requires sophisticated analysis of successive mapshots, and the ability to attribute action sequences to perceived agents is fundamental to interagent programming.

In biological evolution, the development of interagent programming involving action attribution of any sophisticated kind follows long after mere agent recognition. Sexual reproduction requires some form of agent recognition, but the recognition of an agent as an object type doesn't require much in the way of agency attribution. However, if we want to keep up some illusion of simulating the biological evolution of cognition, we will add a reproductive clock to the body of our agent. The environment will include some other agent of the same model physical type as our agent. (Of course, we need not give the other agent a complete and independently functioning cognitive program; we need only give it some appropriate mobility. Later this agent will receive input from a human operator of the program and will indeed be seen to act in as full-fledged a way as any agent might act in this environment, given the constraints of its body.) When the reproductive clock rings, our agent may search out the other agent and engage in a reproductive routine with it. The model physical consequences of reproduction need not particularly concern us.

Once agent recognition is in place along with the analysis of successive mapshots, we can begin to describe the processes of interagent functioning. For the remainder of this section we will concern ourselves with prelinguistic aspects of interagent attributions.

Prelinguistic Interagency Attribution

Action Analysis

We begin by giving our agent a series, indefinite in number, of *agent files*. For simplicity, our world will contain only two agents; and thus our agent will only use two: *Agent-1 file* and *Agent-2 file*. The Agent-1 file contains our agent's representation of its own states — that is, its own perceptions, goals, current and past maps, current and past actions, and so on. The Agent-2 file contains our agent's representation of the states of the other agent: the other agent's perceptions, probable current map, probable current action, probable current goal, and so on. At the outset, of course, both files are empty. We may allow that the Agent-1 file corresponds so exactly to the cognitive system employed by our agent that the very processes themselves as they occur are immediately filtered off for representation in the Agent-1 file just prior to their primary use in cognition. Thus within the Agent-1 file will be temporally coded maps, a current causal list, current hypotheses, a current dominant goal, and time-coded current and recent actions. The Agent-2 file may itself be part of the Agent-1 file since, in that way, it is clear that whatever is in the Agent-2 file is an attribution by Agent-1 to Agent-2.

We must now frame some system for connecting perception to action attribution. We will allow that Agent-2 is perceived to be in any one of a finite number of possible states. The variables are: the location the agent occupies; the position of its locomotor (i.e., locomotor engaged or locomotor static); the position of its grasper (i.e., grasper grasping, or grasper open); the orientation of the agent within the location; the position of its perceiver (i.e., perceiver perceiving, or perceiver shut); the orientation of its perceiver relative to the body of the agent (which yields the angle of perception); the position of the ingest functor (i.e., engaged or unengaged); the state of the affect marker (i.e., smile, neutral, or frown); and the state of various other marker slots (for example, hunger marker on or off).

Given such a listing from perception of Agent-2's current state, an analysis of successive mapshots is possible showing Agent-2 as hungry and as locomoting in direction such and such. Such analysis, of course, would not take place during dreaming but would be attendant upon the events themselves. Based upon such initial analysis, deeper analysis linking the locomotion to the hunger marker, for example, can be undertaken. (For a discussion related to the sort of action-extraction analysis contemplated below, see Salveter 1979.)

Of the variables involved in determining the state of Agent-2 at the level of immediate perceptual interpretation, the one that might seem most foreign or overly cognitivized — impure to use our earlier nomenclature — is a goal-marker such as hunger-on. One might object, for example, that neither humans nor animals have any such goal-markers. However, (1) we can easily imagine a world in which goal-markers were as perceptible as Frown and Smile are for human interagency; and (2) there are markers of Fear in humans and other animals. People who are hungry do have a certain look about them. People who are lusting for sex may also have a certain look, and it's not quite the hungry-for-food look. Animals exude different chemicals when in different motivational states, arch their backs in characteristic ways, and wag their tails in characteristic ways: these events give away the current motivational state of the beast. And (3) even without clear goal-markers, the construction of goal-hypothesis programs could be undertaken based only on the more general affect markers, Smile, Frown, and Neutral, and the various locomotive, grasping, reproductive, and ingesting goings on that would result from the analysis of successive mapshots. The inclusion of goal-markers is thus both warranted and in any case dispensable in a more sophisticated program.

Finally, a system of action analysis at a number of deeper levels will be provided to the agent. The agent has a number of initial scripts that it uses to satisfy its current dominant goal. It has access to representations of these scripts and interprets actions of Agent-2 according to the patterns provided by the scripts. Its representations of its scripts are given in formats such as those described below.

Of course, the attribution of purposes and the interpretation of actions of another agent have function apart from their role in laying the base for the acquisition of language. We will now see how a number of prelinguistic interagent activities can take place within an action-interpretation system such as that just been alluded to.

There are only so many possible mapshots and, therefore, only so many possible segments of a map — in other words, only so many possible states of affairs to be perceived.

Information in mapshots may be extracted by the epistemic system in the form of propositions in the following way: The epistemic system is informed with a propositional calculus to operate on information extracted in this format. Propositions about mapshots are assigned values True, False, and Possible. (Possible is assigned when the proposition cannot be assigned either True or False.)

Primary Mapshot Propositions

Propositions extracted from single mapshots are of a fixed finite number of types. For example, there are propositions stating what object is at what location in the mapshot: "$T_n O_n L_n$." And there are propositions stating the relative positions of one object to another, as in "F at L_6 W_2 A at L_8," which states that the food at L_6 is two locations West of the agent at L_8. Obviously, the value of any primary mapshot proposition of these sorts can be assigned by direct consultation of the information in the mapshot.

A more interesting primary mapshot proposition concerns other agent perception, such as "At T_n A_2 Perceives F at L_6." We allow that this proposition is derived as true from "At T_n A_2 at L_5 Perceiver oriented West; and F at L_6" (so long as the map works out such that, when A is at L_5 and its perceiver is oriented West, then whatever is at L_6 will be in its field of perception). To the objection that this leaves no room for erroneous attribution of perception to other agents, we reply, "What if a duckling imprints on a mouse?" In other words, prelinguistic systems of judgment of this kind are still part of the bootstrapping of cognition. There is plenty of room in which to build more sophisticated systems of judgment in language — systems of judgment that will render these occasionally erroneous judgments beside the point even if they continue to be made, or will ensure that there is a point of entry back into these judgments to prevent them from being made.

Multiple Mapshot Interpretation: First Level

The interpretation of more than one mapshot so as to derive propositional content from them is done at a series of levels. At the first level, only two mapshots are compared and content is extracted from them in propositional form. From two consecutive mapshots can be derived propositions concerning the *motion of nonagent objects*, the *locomotion of agents* from one location to its adjacent neighbor, the *grasping* on the part of some agent of some object, the *ingesting* of some object by some agent, and, if we wish to add these to our agent-states descriptions and environmental causal laws, *expelling* some object and *producing a sound*.

Also at the first level of interpretation from two consecutive mapshots are the *causal assertions* concerning facts such as locomotion, grasping, ingesting, and so on. The agent at Location-6 oriented West with locomotor engaged is in a physical state whose causal consequent is the subsequent state of affairs in which the agent is at Location-5 (one location West of 6) with locomotor engaged. This causal statement captures the fact that it is the environment program which relates one mapshot to its successor through the model rules of physical causation.

The connection between 'the mind' of the agent and its body happens in the interval between the successive states recorded by an agent at mapshots. Thus cognitive events determine successive physical states of the agent, given other facts about the environment, such as whether the relevant adjacent location is vacant.

From two mapshots, the causal version of the appearance of food from seed in the appropriately fertile area can be deduced. Once our agent has listed the cause of the appearance of food as the presence of seed in the appropriate area, our agent will be able both to analyze successive mapshots in which food appears in this way and to state the occurrence as falling under the causal law that it has discovered.

Multiple Mapshot Interpretation: Second Level

At the second level of interpretation, propositions are extracted from propositions derived from multiple mapshot interpretation at the first level. Alternatively, they can be interpretations of the patterns of mapshot pairs. These patterns are innately given in the form of initial scripts or fragments of initial scripts; or they are the result of an *Agent-2 behavior analyzer*, which scans the sequences in which Agent-2 plays a part and extracts the routinized script patterns that underlie the behavior (via procedures such as thse discussed in Dietterich and Michalski 1981); or they are the result of a *planner or script constructor*. The planner or script constructor calculates the outcomes of sequences of smaller routines or scripts and evaluates these outcomes with regard to its various goals. The planner representations will thus be phrased in a patterned activity or script form that could be applied in the interpretation of Agent-2 activity at the second level of interpretation. Through one route or another, concepts such as TRANSPORT or, in Schank's vocabulary, PTRANS can be applied in mapshot interpretation at level-2, so that the proposition that Agent-2 transported Object-food from L-4 to L-10 during the interval t-2568 to t-3574 might be expressed. (Some of the formal tools powerful enough to represent such propositions have been developed, for example, in Schank's conceptual dependency theory even in its earlier forms, and recently in a more general form than is required for our model world, in Allen 1984.) Similarly, a running *current state analysis* might be maintained featuring concepts such as "No danger present. Agent-2 present; Agent-2 locomoting toward food; Agent-1 observing Agent-2."

Multiple Mapshot Interpretation: Third Level

At this level, interpretations are made with regard to the purposes or goals of Agent-2 that its second-level activities, such as *transporting seed*, are intended to fulfill. For example, if Agent-2 has been observed transporting seed into the area of the space believed by Agent-1 to be *fertile* — that is, the location identified as part of the causal story behind the appearance of food — then Agent-1 might make the hypothesis that Agent-2 has the plan of making food. If, however, the transportation of seed is associated in a larger sequence with the creation of a *wall* against predators, then its purpose is different from that of creating food or at least serves several purposes rather than one. The interpretation of mapshot sequences as embodying the activities of Agent-2 in the fulfillment of such purposes — stopping predators and making food, for example — requires the attribution of beliefs and plans by Agent-1, to Agent-2, the agent Agent-1 perceives in the environment.

The Attribution of Beliefs

In order for Agent-1 to be building a wall against predators behind which Agent-2 might rest, Agent-1, will have to represent Agent-2 as having the belief, among others, that if a predator encounters a wall it will not come past it; as having the goal of avoiding predators in general; and as having the specific intention of doing something to fulfill the goal through this action.

Of course, there must be a connection between the sequence of mapshots recorded by Agent-1 and the attribution of beliefs to a second agent. The grounds upon which the belief is assigned or attributed to Agent-2 must be present in Agent-1's mapshot sequences. The simpler the model world and the simpler the belief, the easier it is to see how a program might be constructed that enables such attributions to be made based on the contents of sequences of mapshots. Minimally, such a program will feature concepts roughly like the following:

> A-2 believes P if and only if A-2 has mapshots from which P can be derived by an agent with the interpretive procedures of A-1; *and* A-2 has in fact made the derivation.

Agent-1 may well have information concerning what A-2 has seen, or what perceptions and hence mapshots it attributes to A-2, and it therefore may well be able to judge that A-2 is in a position to derive the proposition in question. The evidence that it has in fact made the derivation is precisely that its action is action that would emerge from our agent's script constructor or planner, based on that belief and on such an environmental configuration.

The attribution of intention follows a similar route. An agent has an intention to do X where 'X' is a plan or script expressed in the appropriate formalism, if and only if the agent has constructed the plan or script, has applied it in its abstract form or pattern to the situation present to it, has tested it for the likely outcome of this application, has tested the outcome against its current highest purposes positively, and has entered the first step of the plan or script as the next act in the executor-functor that leads to the motor equipment. As with belief attributions to other agents, the attribution of intentions to other agents cannot be done except on the assumption that the pattern of activity of Agent-2's fitting the having of the intention is evidence for the attribution of the intention. The evidence that Agent-2 intended to do something is in the structure of what Agent-2 has been perceived as doing. (Nor would one expect there to be any other kind of evidence for attribution of intentions; and if there has to be some other kind of evidence, then a pure model of rational agency is impossible.) And the organizing principle of such structuring is in the general assumption that Agent-2 is built along similar lines as Agent-1. The basic mirroring of agency is fundamental to the construction of a pure model of rational agency.

Cooperation and Competition

Although the modelling of cooperation and competition is not vital to the construction of a pure prelinguistic model of agency, it is nevertheless interesting to note that the basis for the concepts of cooperation and competition, or helping and hindering, are present in any such model. For with the attribution of goals to another agent, any action undertaken by the first agent can be assessed as negative or position with regard to its contributions to the satisfaction of the goals of the other agent, and can therefore be assigned a value as a cooperative or competitive action.

There is thus the possibility of designing a theme tracker or character modeller that assigns cooperative and competitive values to the activities of the other agent, differentiates between situations in which cooperation predominates and situations in which competition predominates, and further adjusts its own behavior in ways that conform to the balances the other agent has struck. In this way an agent at various stages in its career might adopt another agent as a mentor on fundamental styles of behavior. Such a program is no doubt beyond us at the moment, but the fact that we can outline in pretty clear terms what it is meant to accomplish, and can see it as an extension of the sorts of programs that are already practical, is encouraging. (For a related discussion of program tiers, see Schank and Abelson 1977.)

Over the long term, then, the modelling of character development need not defy computational analysis. And in a more immediately practical range of research, we can see how a pure model agent might be designed that arbitrarily oscillates between being cooperative and being competitive within a certain range of its options. It might even appear to have moods.

Language Acquisition

Our task in this section is to demonstrate that a system such as that was sketched out above can be augmented by a number of other units, so that the system taken as a whole is not only a survivor, mapmaker, causal analyzer, and other agent interactor but also a language learner and communicator. We want to be able to look at the language-acquisition system in sufficient detail that we can see how it would be possible, and feasible given our current programming abilities, to give Agent-1 the option when hungry, say, of either finding food efficiently on its own, as it was able to do via the devices given it so far, or of finding another agent and asking the other agent where food is, or commanding or requesting that the other agent find food and bring it to Agent-1. A crucial requirement is that all the words that Agent-1 uses are words that Agent-1 has acquired through a natural process from another agent — in this case, from an actual human instructor interacting with Agent-1 via the representation of Agent-2. Agent-1 may not begin with knowledge of any terms of human language. Agent-1 may begin only with a language-learning system which enables it to acquire words from the other agents it interacts with — in this case the human operator who controls the movements of Agent-2 whose movements are then perceivable by Agent-1. In this way, the Agent-1 program is kept entirely pure in the sense earlier introduced. All of the information received by Agent-1 concerning the doings of the other agent is in the first instance received in the 'raw' model perceptual format.

It is, I believe, the fact that no pure microworld interagency programming has thus far been attempted that accounts for the lack, to date, of a program that attempts to simulate language acquisition from the base up. First-word learning involves environmental exchange and interagency exchange, and thus can be modelled only within a pure program of some sort. Given the enormous problems presented by pure real-world knowledge representation, pure microworld programming is the practical route to follow. The interagency attributions might be circumvented in various ways during the bootstrapping phase of language acquisition. But since these very attributions will be needed and may not be circumvented for the modelling of genuine language use and rationality, and since it is harder to circumvent them for language acquisition than to use them, and since the more language acquisition is brought within the representational framework of rationality the more successful the illusion of consciousness is likely to be evidenced in the behavior of the device during language acquisition as well as language use and prelinguistic purposive behavior, the obvious choice is to try to provide a sketch of some elements of a pure microworld interagency approach to the modelling of language acquisition.

In the previous section we discovered how, in essence, the sorts of formal elements that can be used both in the operation of the planner and in the representations of propositional content eventually to be the basis for language can also be the representations of the states of affairs or configurations of mapshots, either singly or in sequence, organized according to agent activity, causal relationships, spatial relationships, temporal relations, and so on. In the literature on this subject, two out of three corners of this triangle have been joined: linguistic representation and problem solving. (See, for example, Charniak 1981.)

There seems to be no reason a single formal system cannot also serve for the propositional content extracted from a model environment. If it can serve as such, the language-acquisition device already has what it fundamentally needs, insofar as representational systems are concerned. The contents of the language-acquisition device, then, are a matter of linguistic bootstrapping tactics. If the outlines of the previous sections are correct, then the programmer's ultimate resort in solving unexpected complexities to keep the program design moving forward — namely, simplifying the environment to the point where the complexity has been simplified out of that world — should not be a necessary ploy here.

In general design, there is a lexicon with, so to speak, two columns: the prelinguistic representations used by the planner, and action extraction program, and so forth, , on the one side, and the blanks that, as the use of the program progresses, gradually fill up with the words of a natural language on the other.

Our first task is to see how the lexicon's right-hand side can get filled up. In a rough and ready way, we will take our cue from one of the more obvious features of human first-language acquisition. We'll start with learning to name objects. The activities involved here are:

1. Confirming mutual attentiveness
2. Establishing the communication floor
3. Extracting the action: Agent-2 is showing Agent-1 an object

4. Extracting a possible *name* of the object that Agent-1 is being shown
5. Testing the hypothesis of '4'
6. If successful, entering the name into the lexicon

Since the first words learned by children tend to be words referring to spatio-temporal objects in their presence (Schlesinger 1982, Chapter 5; Anglin 1977), we begin with this process. Although the modelling of referent pairing in early language acquisition is enormously complex for humans, there is nothing to suggest that a suitable idealization of referent pairing appropriate to a given microworld cannot be functionally modelled.

Mutual Attentiveness

The visual channel in humans is dominant in establishing communication contexts (Schaffer 1977; Urwin 1978), and there is no reason we should not attempt to model mutual attentiveness through our model visual perception. (The perception we've given Agent-1 is a model of visual perception because Agent-1 perceives configurative object states at a distance.)

Mutual attentiveness in a system such as the one we have developed so far involves Agent-1's attribution to Agent-2 that Agent-2 is attending to Agent-1, and Agent-1's attribution to Agent-1 that Agent-1 is attending to Agent-2. Such a representation might be taken to follow from a sufficient number of successive mapshots in which the two agents' perceivers have each other in their respective ranges.

We will also allow that mutual attentiveness sets Agent-1 up for *communication readiness*, which, when the lexicon is not yet complete, will entail *word learning readiness*. In the absence of danger or hunger, then, the only Explore activity will be that of language learning or use.

Establishing the Communication Floor

In humans and mammals there are all sorts of subtle cues that enable one of the two partners in an interactive situation to take the lead to establish a communication floor. As Newson (1978) points out, if communication is to be able to take place, the individuals involved in the communication must be capable of performing role-trading actions within which the vehicles of communication will be given. This very role trading process can be, and in fact is, abstractly rehearsed.

For our purposes we can distinguish between two modes of establishing the communication floor: *relinquishing* and *negotiating*. Until the lexicon is sufficiently filled, mutual attentiveness can normally be followed by relinquishing the communication floor. However, negotiating for the floor will be involved in testing for the hypothesis of a particular name. We will return to the negotiating mode when we deal more specifically with that phase.

Extracting the Act of Being Shown an Object

Perhaps the simplest model act of showing would be one that involves transporting an object from a large distance away from Agent-1 to within a narrowly defined range of proximity to Agent-1. But there are other methods of showing something. We can point to an object and check to make sure that the person we're communicating with ends up looking not at the finger doing the pointing but at the object being pointed to. Whatever the method of showing, the underlying structure of this action involves the doing of something that causes the other agent to attend to the object being shown. The human language-acquisition device may well be flexible enough to use referent pairing as part of the means of identifying acts of showing. For our purposes, though, we need not model so flexible a device. Rather, it is sufficient that we establish a set of possible SHOW options along with the attribution form: Agent-A DOES D, Planning that Agent-B will attend to Object O. As a consequence, there will be several action patterns that when Agent-1 extracts them from Agent-2's behavior, immediately alert Agent-1 to the possibility that Agent-2 is SHOWing Agent-1 an object. These action patterns, of course, must be designed in such a way that it would be natural for the human operator of Agent-2 to create them when the human operator of Agent-2 is trying to show Agent-1 an object in the microworld.

Extracting a Possible Name

Let's now assume that Agent-1 has been shown an object and has extracted: Agent-2 SHOW Agent-1 Object F_n - L_n during T_n - T_o. The mutual attentiveness will have triggered the acquisition system to take note of the action patterns, and the SHOW act will further alert the language-acquisition device to be on the alert for a name or, more accurately, an act of NAMEing.

To name something is to do something that causes an agent who is believed by the naming agent to not have the name already entered in its lexicon, to list in its representation of the lexicon of the agent doing the naming the symbol that is the name next to the lexical representation of the object (or, at the start, the type of object) being named. We can be fairly crude about this, however, and let the agent assume that the lexicon it constructs is the common lexicon, so that anything that is entered into its representation of Agent-2's lexicon is automatically entered into its own lexicon as well.

The simplest act of naming is the production of a perceptible, which is the token of a type that constitutes the name. The extraction of the symbol that is meant to be the name is thus the next task. How does Agent-1 know what a symbol is? Two approaches might be given here: First, any configuration of a set of elements that provides a certain degree of variation possible within a range might be construed as providing a set of symbols. This approach allows for maximum flexibility. The second approach is to assume that first language-learning with Agent-1 must come through a certain channel: auditory stimuli, say. It follows that a 'deaf Agent-1 baby' would never be able to learn a language. This approach, then, would definitely differ from the human situation. But surely deprivations exist that would make it impossible for a human to learn language. If a baby had no taste, touch, sight, or hearing, could it learn to communicate via smell only? The answer is, I think, not obvious. For simplicity, let's assume that in Agent-1's world the only things that, in the *first instances of language acquisition*, can count as symbols come in an audial or model sound channel.

Next we can assume that the phonological units of the sound channel are discrete and discretely recognizable innately by Agent-1. Once again there is a high degree of adaptation that matches Agent-1's world to Agent-1. A particular phonological system would have to be chosen for the model environment and Agent-1's innate audial interpretive system, but this task is hardly forbidding. There is no need for elaborate specifics here, but I will introduce examples as we need them. In each case the assumption will be that the phonological aspect conforms to the model phonological patterns of Agent-1's interpretive system.

We will also assume that the production of sound is made by some perceptible motor behavior, such that a single mapshot will show a vocalizer engaged or a vocalizer unengaged, and a double mapshot first-level interpretation will yield the information that vocalization has taken place, and identify which phoneme has been produced. There may or may not, then, be a need for a second sensory perceptual channel for Agent-1 whereby it hears the sound without having to lip-read the vocalizer so to speak. There are obvious advantages to the double-channel system: Attention need not switch back and forth so much; and as only agents may be capable of making sounds in this world, the language learning will take immediate note of sound production.

Our next question concerns the way in which Agent-1 comes to assume that a symbolic output of Agent-2 in the auditory channel has come to an end. For our purposes a pause of a sufficient length following symbolic output (sound production) can cue the end of the symbol. (For a discussion of the variety of intonational and junctural cues to sentence boundaries, see Lehiste 1970.)

In effect, then, there will be sequences of events in which Agent-2 calls the attention of Agent-1 in the inaugurate communication way, brings an object from outside a certain proximity to Agent-1 to within that proximity to Agent-1, and then produces a set of audial phonemes followed by a pause. Agent-1 will record this event as Agent-2 showing the object to Agent-1, and it will construct the hypothesis that the symbol string is to be entered in the empty lexicon as the 'name' for the object just shown.

If we follow the human situation and expect that Agent-2 will be quite loose in the means by which it goes about teaching language to Agent-1, the symbolic trains following actions whereby bits of food are shown to Agent-1 might be something like "This is food" or "Food" or "Yummy" or "Do you want any food?" It is only natural to assume that a whole batch of entries will get stored initially in the lexicon next to the prelinguistic internal representation Food. Then there will be a simplifier whereby the most frequent or salient element is extracted for a serious hypothesis. From the previous list the abductive program might yield two names for food, namely 'food' and 'yummy' (the latter, moreover, might eventually get refined down to 'yum' if 'yum yum' and the like is also produced by Agent-2 in a naming way.) The lexicon, of course, will be a file constructed in such a way as to be able to accommodate a list of entries with no principled limit.

Confirming Hypotheses

Assuming that Agent-1 has made a tentative entry in the lexicon for food, say, it must now have some methods of confirming or disconfirming its hypothesis. Let's say Agent-1 has made the hypothesis that 'is food' is a name of food. (It might have 'concluded' as much because Agent-2 kept saying things like "That-is-food," and "Here-is-food.") Roughly speaking, Agent-1 will have to confirm this 'conclusion' by using the name and waiting for the appropriate reaction. If Agent-2 shows approval, Agent-1 will continue to operate in keeping with the hypothesis; if Agent-2 shows disapproval, Agent-1 will suspend the hypothesis until further data come in.

Involved in this process is the action concept, *test* hypothesis. The lexicon, then, will have a *hypothesis only* marker as opposed to a *confirmed* marker. An entry bearing the 'h' marker will get tested at an early opportunity.

To test a hypothesis, Agent-1 should first try to obtain the attention of Agent-2; that is, in the terms set up thus far, it will *inaugurate communication.*

What Agent-1 will have in mind to do next is to show Agent-2 the object whose referring word or name Agent-1 has just tentatively listed subject to confirmation. It will then produce the word, record Agent-2's reaction, and assess the hypothesis.

But what if Agent-2 doesn't wait for Agent-1 to show the object? What if Agent-2 immediately begins, say, to show Agent-1 some other object, with a view to producing a symbol for it and teaching that to Agent-1. Or what if Agent-1 misperceives the successive eye contact mapshots as communication readiness, when Agent-2 has no intention to inaugurate communication while, say, the human operating Agent-2 simply was daydreaming, or went out of the lab to get a sandwich, and left Agent-2's representation idle?

After judging that Agent-2 and Agent-1 are in a state of communication readiness, Agent-1 must now negotiate for time to initiate communication or to assess the success of its initiation of communication. A determination must be made as to which agent in the situation is actually managing to hold the communication power balance and can successfully take hold of the communication floor. The notion of holding the floor in group meetings thus seems to be a formal extension of a notion basic to all communication situations. Even imitation games between infant and mother imply the trading of a communication floor (Newson 1978).

Negotiating for the Communication Floor

Negotiating for a communication floor resembles jockeying for an opening in a sparring match. Just as establishing communication readiness through eye contact may be an evolutionary build from eye contact made, say, during the battles of stags or at the beginning of a staring match or possible fight by two cats, so it is that negotiating the communication floor may be an evolutionary development from negotiating for the first move of a fight, as in the fight for territory, and a game, as in a mating game. If we had taken the trouble to impart territorial and dominance dispositions to Agent-1, we might find that the development of these concepts bear direct links to the concepts involved in negotiating a communication floor. (Plooij 1978, p. 123, is suggestive in this regard.)

But how to model such negotiation in our model environment? Fixing the specifics would be challenging, but there is nothing quixotic about the attempt to do so in a way that seems both natural for the human operating the Agent-2 and yet determinate for Agent-1 so that it could enter the outcome in the appropriate slot in a way that matches with reasonable frequency the human's representation of the outcome. In the simplest version, Agent-1 could wait for Agent-2 to move, failing which Agent-1 would inaugurate its message. Add to this a monitor that checks for Agent-2's having begun its message together with Agent-1, along with an arbitrary decision in such cases as to whether to continue or to stop. If Agent-2 continues, and Agent-1 continues, then sooner or later one or the other of the two will stop. This conclusion follows statistically, given the randomizer for Agent-1 and given human nature with respect to the operator of Agent-2. If inconclusive negotiation has gone on for a sufficient length of time, then Agent-1 will know to start the message all over again. In fact, this could be standard as soon as some overlap occurs between Agent-1 and Agent-2.

In this manner, Agent-1 is sometimes able to establish the communication floor. What does Agent-1 do with it? Agent-1 proceeds to SHOW Agent-2 the object whose referring name is being tested, and to produce the sounds that make up the word. The order of these two events is random, but there may be a tendency to show first and then to produce the word. Depending how many instruments have been filled in for SHOW, there will be a number of ways of showing an object. In any case, Agent-1 should in principle be able to show Agent-2 anything that Agent-2 can show Agent-1 in the same way that Agent-2 showed Agent-1 the object. Agent-1, then, finds some way of calling the attention of Agent-2 away from something else and to the object. Agent-1 tests to make sure that the method worked, and that Agent-2's attention, for a sufficient hold of successive mapshots, was placed toward the object. Agent-1 then pronounces the word being tested.

Assessing Agent-2's Reaction

Agent-1's attention has been alternating from Agent-2 to the object and back to Agent-2, as required for the act of showing an object to another agent. Now Agent-1 attends to Agent-2 with a view to assessing Agent-2's response to Agent-1's act of showing the object and producing the word being tested as the name.

Assent, pleasure, or approval is what Agent-1 is looking for from Agent-2. Whatever the *approval* concept is, it will at least involve the notion of satisfaction, where satisfaction is a state an agent is in on the point of relinquishing a goal whose object has been provided. The recognition by one agent of the satisfaction of another agent has to come through some expression of satisfaction.

It could come through recognition of complex responses. But we can speed things up immeasurably by assuming that there is a mark of sat-

isfaction. The obvious candidate for this is the *smile* response introduced earlier on in our description of Agent-1. Let us now provide that
Agent-1 innately recognizes the smile feature as a mark of satisfaction.

In simple terms, Agent-1 now looks for a mark of satisfaction that, at
the early language learning phase of its cognitive career, will inevitably
be or include a *smile*. Agent-1 waits to see if Agent-2 smiles or not.

How long should Agent-1 wait for the smile? Perhaps one key
element here is structural rather than temporal: that is, Agent-1 studies
how many and what types of actions by Agent-2 intervene between
Agent-1's action TEST NAME and the occurrence of a smile. The more
intervention, the less Agent-2's smile is interpreted as the response to
Agent-1's act. In addition, there should probably be a temporal threshold within which Agent-1 interprets the smile as a response to Agent-
1's act. This threshold would presumably be narrow enough to allow
Agent-2 only a few intervening acts.

Note that it may be a good idea for the programmer to have a special
set of buttons or levers for the human operator of Agent-2 to use as
express pleasure. The human operator of Agent-2 would probably find it
more natural and easier to remember to push a 'feel pleasure lever' than
to remember to put a smile on the Agent-2 representation, especially
when the screen seen by the Agent-2 operator has the visual field of
Agent-2, which would not include the appearance of Agent-2 at all, and
so wouldn't include Agent-2's smile. But perhaps a little 'reflector box'
could show Agent-2's appearance to the human operator of Agent-2.
People, after all, do know whether they're smiling or not even if they
don't see the smile. The reflector box would compensate for the difficulty of representing tactility on a screen.

By some interpretive guidelines of the form just sketched, sequences
of events will occur that Agent-1 will interpret as:

Agent-2 SHOW O_x Agent-1 and Agent-2 Produce Symbol S_x
    Agent-2 Name O_x: S_x -Hyp.

And:

Agent-1 SHOW O_x Agent-2 and Agent-1 Produce Symbol S_x
    and Agent-2 SMILE = Agent-2 APPROVE: = Agent-2
    APPROVE Hyp.

Here we have used the act concept APPROVE, which was only
briefly touched upon earlier. We have also used the 'hyp.' (or 'hypothesis') marker. Let's look at these in turn.

The *approval* that Agent-1 attributes to Agent-2 is not a primitive act
concept but rather is compounded out of the more elementary concepts

'mark' or 'express' and 'satisfaction'.

Mark or Express

'Mark' or 'express' is also compound, even though it's hard at first to imagine how this can be so. To mark or express is to token a state of affairs; 'tokening' is 'marking' for all intents and purposes. But to mark or token is to cause an object of a certain kind to appear — namely, an object that bears a relation of a certain kind to some entity or state of affairs in the world. That relation is one of conventional or non-natural representation. To mark something is to DO something with the PLAN such that another agent PERCEIVES the DOing and makes various entries *both* in its file of the DOing agent and in its own file. To take another agent to be marking something is to take that agent to have a complex PLAN, and to attribute that PLAN to that agent. In this case the DOing is SMILE, and SMILE immediately calls forth the hypothesis that the SMILEing agent is marking the satisfaction of some goal. In non-communication situations, the disappearance of other goal-markers will aid in the interpretation of the goal that has been satisfied. But in the communication situation, the goal will be one of communication; that is, the goal will be one of having the audience agent make various entries in its mental files. In the language-learning situation, SMILE is taken to token satisfaction that the prior NAME act was correctly grasped — in other words, that a sign was correctly entered as a name.

As far as the hypothesis construction and refinement is concerned, we cannot be sure, in advance of empirical testing with human operators of Agent-2 and in the absence of specific input-device hardware for the operator of Agent-2, as to how well the SMILE mark would work as an accurate indicator for Agent-1. Thus we also cannot be certain as to how many trials Agent-1 should expect to make in confirmation of a name.

Making the Entry

When a sufficient number of tests have resulted in firming up the hypothesis, Agent-1 will enter the word in the lexicon for use. It is hard, prior to the creation of specific versions of the microworld, the representation program, the Agent-1 program, and other aspects of the system, to know how flexible the lexicon must remain for refinements: no is it possible to know how accommodating human operators of Agent-2 will be to Agent-1's anomalies. One suspects that human operators will be highly tolerant of the errors of Agent-1, just as parents are tolerant of the oddities of their children's first words in matters of semantics, pronunciation and grammar. Humans would likely develop some aspects of baby talk in working with Agent-1; they may also engage in the many special forms of discourse found in adult-child speech as opposed to adult-adult speech. (See de Villiers and de Villiers 1978, pp. 192-198, for a summary of adult-child special features of discourse.)

We can assume that the human operator of Agent-2 will not proceed by instructing Agent-1 in a full set of nominals, and only then go on to instruct Agent-1 in the use of these nominals in sentences. Rather, if the human operator of Agent-2 proceeds in the fashion of a parent instructing a child, sentential language games will likely be played with the grasped nominals pretty much from the beginning. Indeed, some nouns are learned through direct referent pairing, and some through sentential language games involving contrastive verbal ostension (Carey 1978; Schlesinger 1982). Our main interest, however, will be in showing how sentential language games may result in the learning of verbs; imperative, interrogative, and assertion markers; negation marker; and other non-nominal parts of speech. The following sections take up these topics. The expectation is that through the learning of elementary verbs and other non-nominal parts of speech, a rich enough semantic base will be created such that language use, which is or might be independently purposive and yet encased in the appropriate interagency attributions, might be engaged in by Agent-1 with the human operator of Agent-2 through his or her representation, Agent-2.

The essential problem here is to move from reference pairing to sentential interpretation. Even the simplest sentence presumably involves a subject, a predicate, and a speech act. I will assume here that the language-acquisition device needs to be equipped only with three speech act types: question, command, and assert. Other aspects of the speaker's act will be attributed by the hearer to the speaker's goal-related plan and/or convention-establishing plan, as described below. The task of Agent-1's language-acquisition device will be to extract accurate hypotheses concerning question, assertion, and imperative markers, at the same time as it extracts accurate hypotheses about the words of the sentence not already listed. This conception thus requires a distinction between a speech-related plan and a goal-related plan.

A brief comparison between the speech act classification employed here and Searle's (1979) classification is in order. Searle classifies speech acts into five types: assertives, directives, commissives, expressives, and declaratives. The assertive type is common to both classifications. My categories of question and command are subsumed within his class of directives. Although I will not examine the issue at length in this context, my hunch is that the distinction between questions and nonverbal directives (i.e., directives to perform a nonverbal act) is important in terms of the ability to construct a language-using device such as Agent-1 is intended to be. The question-and-answer language game needs special treatment. The speech-plan of a nonverbal directive may have to be filled in with an action-game with specific rules. And the question-and-answer language game can be seen as an action-game with specific rules. But there must be a place for the articulation of those rules: moreover, it would seem that the language-learning device will be greatly advantaged by the availability of those rules and disadvantaged by having to learn them. So the question speech act, one way or another, may as well have an account of its own here.

At the same time, I believe that a device with the capacity to make declaratives, directives (both nonverbal and interrogative), and assertives will also be able to construct verbal but noninterrogative directives (i.e., directives to perform acts of speech such that the directives themselves are not interrogatives) as well as commissives and expressives. And declaratives seem to me to be either acts of showing and naming or acts of showing and naming combined with assertions and directions. Accordingly, it seems to me that showing and convention-establishing acts, together with the sentential or speech acts of asserting, questioning, and directing, will suffice to make possible commissives, expressives, and complex declaratives. If I am wrong in this, then commissives, expressives, and sentential declaratives should receive speech-related plan types of their own. But either way, the point to be emphasized, surely, is the one made by Searle: The number of basic types of things we do with language is very limited — by my reckoning, to two or three plus a conventionalizing act; and by Searle's reckoning, to five. The ways in which we put these basic illocutionary types to use are many, and that has to do with the ways our speech-related plans can fit into goal-related plans.

Speech-Related Plans and Goal-Related Plans

If the notion of a question is to be meaningful, there must be a level at which the intention of the speaker is to have the hearer understand that the speech has the effect of requesting an answer. But if the asking of a question is to be useful, there must be the possibility that the overall plan of the speaker is quite independent of the hearer's providing an answer. Similarly, if the making of an assertion is to be useful, there must be a level at which the speech is to be understood *qua* assertion (i.e., as the transference of information): and there must be the possibility of another level at which the plan of the speaker might be entirely contrary to that of information transference (e.g., that of misleading the hearer). We must distinguish, then, between the structure of the semantic plan, which I am calling the speech-related plan, and the structure of the plan that encloses the making of the speech — that is, the structure of the plan for which the utterance, including the semantic or speech-related plan, is the instrument.

At this point we may pause briefly to compare Austin's distinction between illocutionary and perlocutionary acts in *How to Do Things with Words* (1962), and Davis's revision of it in "Perlocutions" (Davis 1980). Davis shows that Austin's boundary doesn't work. What we're left with is the notion that the perlocutionary act is the achieving of the purpose of an act of communication. In our terms, the achievement of communication is the accomplishment or success of a speech-related plan. But we communicate for our purposes, which are the fulfillment of our goal-related plans. What, then, has become of the illocutionary act? Perhaps we might suggest that the illocutionary act takes place just in case a speech-related plan succeeds; but each illocutionary act has a *way* of being carried out that matches or is a product of the goal-related plan it serves. Say A implores B, "Release the prisoner!" B carries out A's speech-related plan, because B has entered in B's file for A that A has the speech-related plan that B will interpret the utterance as one whose fulfillment is the release of the prisoner by B. The illocutionary act of direction has taken place: Its uptake is B's entering the speech plan. But the fact that it is an act of imploring indicates that it is connected with a goal-related plan, and connected in a certain way — namely, with urgency. This aspect will not be fulfilled by B's taking up the speech-related plan and fulfilling it; B must fulfill the goal-related plan and release the prisoner. The perlocutionary act, then, is the fulfillment of the goal-related plan. The illocutionary act is the fulfillment of the speech-related plan in the way that matches or represents it as a product of the goal-related plan.

We return now to speech-related plans as the focus of language learning. The difference between language-learning strategies and language-use strategies is that the former begin with the form or structure of speech-related plans and try to match those patterns with behavior and bits of the world identified as symbols, some of which are entered in the lexicon, some of which are not, whereas the latter requires the fitting of symbols both into speech-related plans and goal-related plans. Language learning focuses only on the speech-related plans and uses them to make entries into the lexicon.

Roughly, the speech-related plan of a question is as follows: A question is a set of moves by Agent-A such that Agent-A plans that Agent-B attends to the moves; that Agent-B interprets the moves as constituting Q-marker, sentence; that Agent-B calculates the truth value of the sentence when the sentence has no question-blank, or calculates a value of the question-blank if there is one under which the sentence is true; that Agent-B answers by uttering an assertion consisting of the true sentence with blank filled in, or an assertion such that Agent-B's speech-plan includes A's attending to the moves constituting the assertion, such that Agent-A might calculate from the assertion the truth value of the sentence (if it has no question blank) originally posed as a question. In addition, it is part of Agent-A's speech plan in making the question that Agent-B enter this plan in Agent-B's file for Agent-A.

Similarly, the speech-plan of a command is that Agent-B attributes to Agent-A (the issuer of the command) the plan that Agent-B interprets the moves constituting the command as having the structure: command-marker, sentence; and the sentence has (in deep structure) an Agent-B referring term and an action-referring term; that B performs the action referred to by the action referring term; and that B attributes to A the last-mentioned plan.

The speech-plan of an assertion is that Agent-B attributes to Agent-A (the asserter) the plan that Agent-B interprets the moves constituting the assertion as having the structure: assertion-marker, sentence; and that Agent-B enters in Agent-B's file of Agent-A the map-attribution that would make the sentence true; and that Agent-B enters in Agent-B's map the information that would make the sentence true; *and* Agent-A as well holds the plan that Agent-B not only attributes all the above as the plan but also enters in Agent-B's map the information that would make the sentence true.

In even more informal terms, the speech-plan of a question involves a question-and-answer sequence. The speech-plan of a command involves a command-and-execute action sequence. And the speech-plan of an assertion involves a statement-and-acceptance sequence. I take it that speech-plan sequences of this kind are by no means immune from formalization. (See, for example, Cohen and Perrault 1979; and Evans 1985.)

Use of Speech-Related Plans in Language Acquisition

Since language acquisition requires the attribution of approval in some form, it might be said that even language acquisition encases speech in goal-related plans. But the plan that the learner attributes to the teacher is that of the teaching of the terms of the language or, to put it another way, the plan of having the learner complete various speech-related plans. The goal-related plan of a teacher is the completion of a speech-related plan. Accordingly, approval is interpreted as confirming the performance of some behavior as the completion of the speech-related plan of the teacher.

The language-learning strategy, then, is to attribute to some moves symbolic status based on the presence of symbols already entered, to construct speech-related plans consistent with what is already attributed to the other agent, to hypothetically attribute them to the speaker, to compare the behavior that would issue from such plans with the behavior of the other agent for possible matches, to engage in the behavior that would complete the speech-related plan being attributed to the speaker, and to look to a response from the speaker with an approval-marker to confirm the attributed speech-plan. The speech-plans, behaviors, and original symbolic moves are stored for further use, since these sets constitute incrementally determining data for the language-acquisition device.

We may also assume that, just as there is an approval-marker, there will be some disapproval-marker that will indicate the noncompletion of a speech-related plan. It is important, of course, that the disapproval-marker be interpreted appropriately as disapproval of the behavior of the learner agent with regard to the speech-related plan, not with regard to the goal related plan. A negation-marker can be learned independent of a disapproval-marker, and once it is learned, there is no further need of a disapproval-marker for aid in the acquisition of other words and speech act markers.

Some Examples

Agent-2 produces an utterance with 'seed' in it. Agent-1 has already learned 'seed'. Agent-2 does not SHOW a seed to Agent-1. The utterance contains more symbols than 'seed'. Agent-1 may now bring and show seed to Agent-2, or Agent-1 may bring seed to Agent-2, but stop short of showing it to Agent-2. Agent-1 then assesses responses to such action. Agent-2's approval to both responses indiscriminately supports the hypothesis that the message means 'find seed' or 'show seed' or 'where is seed?' (imperative, imperative, and interrogative, respectively). Approval of bringing *and* showing without approval of mere bringing tends to confirm 'show seed'.

Learning speech-markers, of course, is of great assistance in reducing possible speech-act plan interpretations. There is a good deal of evidence that an innate component might be at work in the identification of intonation patterns as indicative of interrogative or assertive (Miller 1979, Chapter 5). It is tempting, therefore, to assist Agent-1 with innate knowledge that rising intonation associates with question, and falling terminal intonation with assertion and command. However, it might be impractical at the outset to build an input device that accepts actual speech from the human operator of Agent-2, and also, perhaps, impractical to ask a relatively untutored human operator of Agent-2 to simulate or represent intonation along with the representation of speech. For such practical reasons alone, it might be best to give the ability to Agent-1 to learn the differences between a question, assertion, and command-marker. That this may be done can be seen from the differences in speech-plan types associated with question, assertion, and command. The speech-plan of the question has the question followed by speech; the speech-plan of the command has the command followed by action; and the speech plan of the assertion is followed by neither.

So, for example, all three — 'question marker', 'what', and 'this' — might be learned together via filling in a question speech-plan once some common noun or name, as we've been calling it, has been acquired. Agent-1 will be on the lookout for Agent-2 speech that is possibly morphemically double (i.e., in which no segment has been acquired as a word) and that is accompanied by the act of showing an object whose name has already been acquired by Agent-1. Agent-1 will then proceed to show the object and speak the name learned together with some apparent or possible morphemic segment of Agent-2's speech, under the hypothesis that Agent-2's speech was the question, "Q-marker, what, this." Agent-1 will then attend Agent-2, looking for confirmation or correction in the form of Agent-2's showing the object again to Agent-1, and uttering what Agent-1 assumes is likely to be the answer to Agent-2's original question. Agent-1's speech is compared with Agent-2's second speech and a hypothesis results that some symbol is the symbol for 'demonstrative'. Agent-1 may further test for the symbol 'what' by using Agent-2's original speech and showing some other object, and may further confirm its speech-plan attribution and hypothesis concerning 'this' if Agent-2 names the second object shown, particularly if this is accompanied by the symbol hypothesis-marked 'demonstrative'. Further, the disappearance of some feature of the original utterance other than 'what' in the answer leads to a hypothesis as to the question-marker. (Compare Macnamara 1986, p. 57; the above treats what he leaves assumed — namely, how a demonstrative can be learned.)

Alternatively, if the input device consists of a body operator and a keyboard that represents Agent-2's speech, it might be possible to include arrow-up, arrow-down, and arrow-horizontal as intonation-markers. Agent-1 might assume that intonation determines speech act, and thus have a head start in making its hypotheses.

Once 'demonstrative' has been securely entered into the lexicon, verbs can be directly taught. Agent-2, operated by the human, might present an utterance with 'this', perform an action, and present a new symbol. Agent-1 will attribute to Agent-2 the plan of showing the action and naming it. And once question-marker and 'what' have been entered, Agent-1 may ask for instruction in both activity words and objects that have not yet been named. This should result in efficient learning of words.

The learning of the demonstrative word also greatly facilitates the learning of a negation-marker. Question-and-answer games may be played in which an object is shown and an incorrect word is produced along with a question-marker; the expectation is that the answer to this question will contain both the incorrect word and the negation-marker. The learning of a negation-marker is, of course, vital if a language is to be capable of serving as a vehicle of rationality, since the capacity to make denials is essential to rational linguistic expression. Further, the availability of the negation-marker greatly facilitates the learning of extension boundaries for complex concepts such as activity concepts.

The self-referring index and an agent's proper name can be learned in the following way: Agent-1 interprets an event as embodying this pattern:

Agent-x SHOW Agent-y. $y = x, x \neq 1$
Agent-x MESSAGE: Unknown Symbol S

This fits the NAMEing pattern, and so the symbol will be entered in the common lexicon. But the lexicon will have space for a proper name for Agent-1 and a proper name for Agent-2; in addition, it will have a slot for the self-referring index. Agent-1 may now check for approval on:

Agent-1 SHOW Agent-1. Agent-1 MESSAGE: S

If this message gets approval then S is tentatively listed as the self-referential index and further checked for confirmation. If it is not approved, then 'S' can be tested as a proper name. Agent-1 shows Agent-2 and utters 'S', and waits for approval, and so on. This account of how the self-referential index may be learned may be compared with Macnamara's treatment of the same topic (Macnamara 1986, Chapter 5). Once again, the area with which he is not concerned is the learning mechanism; and it is the learning mechanism on which this approach focuses. "How did he come to understand that I (me) in his mouth referred to himself? The full answer must include an account of an inductive leap on the basis of a few examples, but induction is not my concern here" (p. 97). On the other hand, the logical resources with which the self-referential index may be represented are his concern. The two elements with which he must contend are the nature of the object being referred to by the index, and the temporality requirements that any correct formula capturing the concept that the index is 'the current speaker, whoever that may be' involve. In the system sketched here, any speech will be represented via a speaker's speech-plan. So no agent will be able to engage in any language use at all without implicitly having the notion of the speaker and without being able to substitute an index. Indeed, our idealization of a world that contains only two possible agents may give a clue as to a possible tiering of speech analysis: Speech-plans are given in terms of Agent-A and Agent-B, and in each instance identities are supplied — for example, Agent-A=Agent-2, Agent-B=Agent-1, and so on. Then 'I' would simply be entered opposite 'Agent-A' in the lexicon. Macnamara's logical resources are thoroughly dissolved in the semantic base and the points of its attachment to the microworld as it is represented.

Abstract Terms

By means similar to those described above, the terms that represent concepts used in propositional representations such as 'locomote', 'ingest', and 'perceive' can be acquired. Again, the strategy is to order the instruction phases so that one new element at a time can be introduced and checked for. For example, once proper names for agents, or indexical referring terms for agents, have been introduced, it becomes possible to teach the word for 'perceive', as the form "Agent-2 S̲ Food," uttered when Agent-2 is holding perception on Food (and where 'Agent-2' has been acquired by Agent-1 as the word for Agent-2) and similar forms, enables Agent-1 to abduct the hypothesis that 'S' is the word or contains the word 'perceive'.

More abstract terms may be taught as well by following an appropriately ordered progression. For example, 'thing' may be taught once agent proper names, and 'food', 'seed', 'predator', 'agent', and other terms have been taught. ('Food', 'seed', and 'predator' are dangerous things to teach, no doubt, until a sufficient amount of cultural norms have been established involving walls of food or houses in which both agents can live in relative ease and without fear.) The word 'cause' may be taught by calling attention to sequences in which seeds cause the appearance of food and then uttering, "Seeds cause food," and so on.

Particularly interesting are the terms of intentionality: 'belief', 'believe', 'intend', 'want'. 'Belief' is probably most easily taught following the verb form 'believe'. 'Believe' should be extractable by the use of perception statements followed by 'believe' statements revolving around more than the object of perception. For example, "Agent-2 sees food . . . Agent-2 believes food here," combined with other implicational sentence sequences such as "Agent-2 brings seed here . . . Seed here causes food here . . . Agent-2 believes food here future".'Belief' can be taught as something an agent *has* when the agent believes. The possessive concept can be given a word via selection games involving an agent's bodily parts. So long as an agent can call another agent's attention to its own bodily parts, it can introduce the possessive via "'Agent-1's locomotor's + SHOW Agent-1's locomotor . . . not Agent-1's locomotor + SHOW Agent-2's locomotor'" and so on. The possessive may then be used to introduce an agent's belief.

Tenses and the terms for temporal order — 'before', 'now', 'later' — must probably be learned before the word for 'intention' can be easily taught, since intentions involve future events. 'Before', 'now', and 'future' can be taught by demonstrating some causal sequence and then engaging in various selection games on states of affairs at different points in the repeated demonstrations. For example, Agent-2 demonstrates the creation of food from seed. Agent-2 says "Now seed here . . . Future food here . . . Now (when food appears) food here . . . Not now seed here . . . Before seed here . . ." and so on. Agent-1's language-acquisition device recognizes these selection patterns and, in any case, would find the concepts corresponding to its pre-linguistic temporal order indices.

Once tense words and/or temporal order indices are in the lexicon, the word 'intends' can be taught. Agent-2 will perform a sequence such as the following, "'Now Agent-2 intends Agent-2 SHOW Agent-1 food' followed by the SHOW act" and so on.

Logical terms such as 'if' and 'then' can be taught with the use of complex intentions. For example, if 'intends' is already learned, then 'if' can be taught using patterns in which Agent-2 asserts Agent-2's intention to do something, 'if' some event takes place. Agent-1 might also confirm a hypothesis concerning 'if' by asserting a causal sequence using 'if' or constructing a question concerning a causal sequence using 'if'.

A Complete Semantic Base?

Because the world in which Agent-1 lives has been highly idealized, the formalisms adequate to represent that world are also highly idealized. The simpler the ontology of a microworld, the simpler the language of thought (Fodor 1975) of a device such as Agent-1, and the more feasible it is to conceive of a language-acquisition device that completes the base lexicon entries. Once basic lexical entries are completed, Agent-1 will be able to communicate any belief that it has about its environment, since all beliefs about spatial and temporal relations, objects, actions, and causes are represented in ways that ultimately cash out as map-state combinatorial possibilities. Although some of the concept-acquisition strategies and formalisms sketched out in the foregoing are speculative and preliminary, there is every reason to believe that a language-acquisition device, a planner, a system of agency representation with semantic plans, a system of world representation, and a propositional calculus can be functionally integrated so as to yield a fully entered base lexicon ready for language use. Before discussing language use, however, we must note language learning beyond the base lexicon.

Language Learning Beyond The Base

Even when the base of the language is complete, learning in language will still occur. This learning comes in two main forms in Agent-1's world. First, there is no principled limit to the size of the lexicon, not only because the same prelinguistic representation may be associated identically with two or more words but also because the concepts that can be formed linking the words acquired during the completion of the base are, so to speak, culturally governed and open-ended in their formation. Even in Agent-1's microworld where there might be limits in practice on what concepts can be formed concerning the static aspects of mapshots, there is no limit to the important and interesting-to-Agent-1 new action concepts that can be learned. There is no limit on the size of an interactive goal plan; there is no limit on the size of the sequence of moves that Agent-A plans for Agent-B to perform (and to attribute to Agent-A as Agent-A's plan for Agent-B). These shared plans or, in effect, file-unions can get indefinitely large.

Second, in addition to concept openness, there is the open-ended learning of syntactic forms. As the syntax of a natural language is always subject to change, there is always the requirement in the formal study of human language acquisition that the language acquisition system be capable of continuous learning of syntax. Our interest here, however, is with the illusion of intentional agency, and so the constraints on linguistic theories of language acquisition considered as part of the study of human cognition do not apply to our enterprise. Rather, the relevant question concerns the relationship between the open-endedness of the syntax of complex sentences deriving from the recursive properties of the syntactic base, on the one hand, and the expressive potential of a language, on the other.

As I have shown elsewhere (Angel 1974), a small set of simple sentence types, with no recursive element in the base will suffice for the full expressive potential of a language such as English. It follows that a system in which we could communicate only by paraphrasing our complex sentences, using only conjunction of simple sentences, would not be found lacking in communicative potential. So the relevant task is not to show how the complex details of natural language syntax may be acquired but, rather, to discover the relevance of syntactic specificity in elementary sentence forms to semantic analysis, to show how an Agent-1 planner might operate to paragraph sentences, and how an Agent-1 language acquisition device might treat cross-sentential reference.

In this sketch of machine-to-human basic interagency attributions, I am assuming that there is a fairly low relevance of natural language syntax for semantic analysis of simple sentences. Like apes, Agent-1 might be free with word order where the human interlocutor is not, and yet both Agent-1 and the human should be able to manage (Lowenthal 1982, pp. 344-345). Similarly, failure to perform obligatory deletion would not obstruct human comprehension of the Agent-1 speech. Moreover, if the initial goal of a programmer of a device such as Agent-1 would be to give Agent-1 the ability to communicate via stage-1 language (Brown 1973), the formalizability of natural language syntax acquisition in humans is hardly relevant. For both stage-1 language and beyond in an artificial device, the acquisition of natural language syntax for recursive embeddings need not be a primary focus. Also, I take it that accounts of semantic bootstrapping (e.g., Pinker 1984) and syntax/semantics autonomy (e.g., Grimshaw 1981) are consistent with this approach.

Finally, if a set of structures such as those proposed for the Agent-1 language-learning program is to be of use not only in consideration of the artistry of *agency illusionism* but also for the study of human cognitive development, it may be that without grappling with a fully integrated system of this kind, no way will be found around what Martin Atkinson calls the theoretical vacuum that has befogged semantics in the last ten or fifteen years (Atkinson 1982, 10.4). Unless attention, belief, desire, and planning are modelled together there will be no foundation formalism to which semantic modelling can attach. And belief or knowledge representation must include action extraction and interagency attribution if the foundation formalism is to be rich enough that it can address the question of semantic representation. In the beginning such human-to-machine integrated models will be a far cry from simulations of human cognition, given the degree of idealization of Agent-1, but Agent-1 may nonetheless give the appearance of rational agency.

Language Use

As already mentioned, language learning does not constitute language use, and having a language-acquisition device of the sort sketched here does not guarantee the ability of its holder to use the symbols acquired. The having of a lexicon recording correspondences between innate representational concepts and the words of a natural language guarantees (in an appropriate system) the ability to express propositional content in the terms of a natural language. But for this to be the *expression* of the system, and not just recognizable by us as the tokens of a system such as we use for expression, the ability of the system's planner to *do* things with these propositions is required. But if, for example, Schank's action concepts enable one to represent an enormous range if not all of human action terms, then showing how these concepts are all represented or representable in our system has suggested how the theoretical basis exists for Agent-1 to be able to represent and hence perform an enormous range of speech acts — conditional on these acts being represented in a format that can be operated on by the planner and interpreted by the motor in the appropriate manner. And the theoretical basis is in place for such common representations. The burden of integration is borne by a system of common representation that accommodates action extraction and interagency attribution.

The program sketched out here is ambitious, and undoubtedly only a concerted effort to pull together an integrated system of this sort will tell the tale regarding its scope and limitations. The reader should also be reminded at this point that several levels of implementation problems exist that need to be solved before an integrated system of this sort can be built. But because the system situates language within action theory, and action representation within a system of model perception of a model world, a model body with model needs, a problem solver, and a motor, a human interacting with such a device via an Agent-2 representation will be able to apply the relevant tests for features referred to earlier as the Grice-Bennett presuppositions of language use and rationality. And the device will pass the tests.

What we will now do is uncover the implications of a system designed to meet the requirements of human-to-machine (or machine-to-human depending how you look at it) interagency attributions for the other grounds of skepticism about our ever coming to have the android problem, as discussed at the outset of the analysis.

4

Defusing Android Skepticism

Let us call a human-to-machine interactive perception-based inter-agency attributive language-learning and -using system of the kind sketched here a system with a 'PAL' (Pure Agency attributive Language-learner). Now if a PAL is buildable, as it would seem to be, would it still have a frame problem? Would it still lack common sense? Would it still lack tacit knowledge? Would there still be a central processing vacuum? And, would its modules be essentially unconnected and unintegrated?

To the extent that a functioning PAL is buildable, these problems, *in some sense*, will have been solved. For the PAL to be functioning, it must have plans that enable it to survive, to get into certain states, and to avoid others. Some of these plans will eventually involve the attribution of agency to another element of its environment and, for example, directive speech acts such as "Bring food." Since its planner is tailored to its world, and its world is as simple as it needs to be for the planner to function, a PAL will have whatever common sense it really needs. Of course, there will be danger in the microworld. Accidents, goofs, or failures to plan correctly will result in the death of the PAL and the consequent erasure of all the acquired knowledge it had. But that's a feature of our world too. So the common sense problem is enormous for any device that has to cope with a world as enormously complex as ours, but it can be wholly or partially dissolved by the ontological simplification of the microworld. One thing the feasibility of a PAL system will show is that the degree of agency complexity modellable is independent of the complexity of the world in which the agent lives.

Conclusion 1: Agency complexity is independent of environmental richness.

Another way to put this is to say that the frame problem may be understood in two ways. On the one hand, it may be thought of as nothing but the numbingly difficult problem of filling in all the tiny interstices in the modelling of the world in which humans live and the modelling of the corresponding PAL units so that simple PALs such as those sketched here can be elaborated into more sophisticated models of human functioning. To understand the frame problem this way is to understand it as nothing but the problem of nudging one's way forward along the continuum, bit by programming bit.

On the other hand, one may understand the frame problem as presenting the programmer with the challenge of programming the unprogrammable. "How can one ever hope to program common sense?" is the question the frame problem is seen as posing in this 'Dreyfusian' way of understanding it. I hope the model of PAL programming accomplishes the dissolution of the second way of understanding the frame problem. What is left is the problem of elaborating PAL models — that is, elaborating environments for PALs and elaborating the competences within the PAL structures. If people did not know how to build a foundation and supporting walls, they might think they had an unsolvable roof problem. Learning how to build a foundation and supporting walls would not solve the many little roof problems, but it would dissolve the unsolvable roof problem — that is, how to get a roof to float on thin air. PAL programming, I suggest, shows that we do not have an unsolvable frame problem, or at least that there is no reason at present to hold that we do, in the same way that presenting a sketch of foundation and supporting wall structures would establish a *prima facie* case that one does not have an unsolvable roof problem.

Roughly the same story may be told about module integration. The hypothesis of a buildable PAL *is* the hypothesis of modules functioning in a sufficiently integrated way to create some degree of language use that fulfills independent-from-other-agent purposes. The addition to Dennett's (1978a) flowchart of action analysis routines, interagency attributive strategies, language acquisition, and a planner that operates to match independent purposes or desires with beliefs so as to issue in acts (curiously missing from Dennett's chart altogether) constitutes the provision of integrating links for an independently purposive language-using system.

What has happened to the problem of integration, then? It appears that integration surfaces as a problem with any system that is not built around independent purpose satisfaction. Conversely, a system that is seen to satisfy independent (i.e., other-agent neutral) purposes is seen to be an integrated system. This doesn't mean that any integrated system will be seen to be a rational agent. To satisfy tests for rationality, the system will have to be capable of making interagency attributions, and using language in its interests. But integration, as a problem, arises through neglect of independent purpose fulfillment.

> *Conclusion 2*: Building independent purposes and interests, as well as interagency competences into a system is vital for the integration of cognitive subsystems.

Thus the unsolvable or baffling frame problem appears when we contemplate AI systems that do not include pure interagency attributive competences. Once our AI systems are integrated around such competences the unsolvable or baffling frame problem disappears and is replaced by whatever questions we have concerning indefinite complexifications. AI boosters will put it this way: To solve the frame problem is to build properly integrated systems — that is, systems with pure interagency attributive competences. Scoffers may find themselves still scoffing at the boosters' attitude toward having located the continuum. But each system properly integrated around purpose satisfactions and interagency attributive competences will not itself be riddled with a frame or integration problem. And whereas it may be appropriate to scoff at the idea that strictly nonconnectionist approaches to the 'complexifications' will suffice to transform a discrete digitalized agent functioning linguistically in a discrete digitalized environment into a fine-grained agent functioning linguistically in a fine-grained environment, the need for neural-net or connectionist realizations of the various units of the agency-attributive language using device does not undercut the boosters' theory that the construction of agency-attributive language-using devices constitutes the location of the continuum. On the contrary. Although connectionists thus far haven't claimed to know how to use connectionism in solving the really difficult AI-cognitive science problems of rational agency, possession of a complete agency-attributive language using computational grid to squeeze neural-net flesh into, if anything, justifies the boosters' approach to the current situation, and may well provide connectionists with something of the framework they are looking for. At any rate, the implementation of an integrated model of agency, the building of a system with a PAL, is a procedure for addressing the frame problem, alias the common sense problem.

It has become fashionable in recent years to describe as the naive period those days when AI microworld programming was believed to hold significant promise for cognitive science. Dreyfus and Dreyfus (1986), for example, mock the continuum hypothesis — that intelligent systems can be built up incrementally so as to come ever closer to match the full range of human cognitive abilities. But as I hope I have shown, integrated PAL modelling locates the continuum. The continuum hypothesis is ripe to waken from its decade-long slumber.

Conclusion 3: An integrated system with a PAL locates the continuum. The onus is on the skeptic to show why all PALs will be unbuildable or, alternatively, if some PALs can be built, to show why the continual elaboration of such a system (including the elaboration of the microworld) cannot proceed indefinitely, leading eventually to a replacement of the microworld by the world.

With the shift of onus back on the skeptic in this way, we can go on to ask the next question, "But *would it be conscious?*"

PART TWO

The Philosopher's Project

5

Rational Agency and Consciousness: Outlining the Argument

"But would it be conscious?"

To begin with, we must clarify what type of device we mean to be considering with respect to the question of its consciousness. For there are, according to one classification schema at any rate, four groups of devices we might be considering here:

Group A: Artificial devices at the level sketched at the end of Part 1, and in environments like those described at the end of Part 1 (each member of which we'll call a 'PAL-1').

Group B: Very much more sophisticated devices than PAL-1s: creatures that can learn much more language than a PAL-1 but which live in an environment not all that much more complex than a PAL-1.

Group C: Linguistically very sophisticated devices that are also capable of living in 'smooth' or 'fine-grained environments' like those of humans rather than the highly restricted digitalized environments of PAL-1s. In Group C, we include only those devices whose competences are very different from humans (they can calculate math problems that no humans can do in their heads, say, while their affective life is poverty-stricken compared to humans).

Group D: Those devices whose specific competences, affective life, and so on, are perfect models of human competences — as perfect as one can envision.

Also, in the case of each group, we may be dealing either with a purely formal realization of the program and a device that lives only in monitors, so to speak, or, we may be dealing with a device that has a physically realized body which functions in a physically realized environment. Thus there are 8 types of creatures we may be asking about. For each of these types of device we want to know the following:

1. Does it matter whether the program is merely formally realized as opposed to actually realized in a physical environment and a physical body?
2. In either case, if it doesn't matter, or in the latter case, if it does matter, is the device in question deserving of moral attitudes? Ought it to bear legal rights? And, most centrally, would it experience *qualia*? That is, would it be a true subject of experience, having true subjective experience, as a human does?

I propose to answer these two questions in sequence. In brief, my argument goes as follows:

1. A human brain hooked up to monitors and interacting with other humans through the other humans' input via a series of Agent-2 devices in the monitors would still be conscious. At least, I anticipate that the reader's intuition would conclude as much. But if so, the burden of consciousness attribution falls on the analysis of the physical device that holds the 'brain' part of the program. Accordingly, nothing much hinges on whether a device of group A, B, C, or D is formally or materially realized.
2. We will adopt full-fledged moral attitudes and grant the objects of those attitudes legal rights only if we attribute to the objects of those attitudes conscious experiences in the sense of having experiences of the quality of objects — that is, only in the sense of having the experience of *qualia*. Thus we need to address the central question of whether the device is a truly experiencing subject or experiences *qualia*. We are sure to disagree about the devices in groups A, B, and C if we do not agree about the devices in group D. So we begin by conceiving of the paradigmatic case of group D: the 'Cyborg', an organic human baby minus its brain into whom a computer-brain has been implanted at birth, and whose life is entirely normal based on all outwardly observable behavioral and dispositional characteristics.

Now, with respect to the Cyborg, the problem of consciousness attribution is a mere instance of the general other-minds problem unless there is some distinctive feature of the way the computer-brain of the Cyborg works compared with the human which makes consciousness attribution to it a special instance of the other-minds problem. Although we can always *imagine* or *conceive* that the device is wholly unconscious (i.e., does not have any experience of *qualia*, is a mere simulation without real intentionality or real consciousness), we nonetheless have no way of identifying whether it is conscious without some general analysis of the type of organization of matter that would be conscious as opposed to the type of organization of matter that would not be conscious.

I suggest that we can *conceive* of a contrast between the type of causal organizations of the Cyborg on the one hand, and that of the human on the other, that would plausibly justify the withholding of consciousness attribution to the Cyborg. But the likelihood of finding such a contrast is either remote in the extreme or incalculable and not worth speculating on at present.

If this position is correct, then, the Cyborg, if it is ever built, would merit consciousness attribution and the bearing of moral and legal rights.

But what of the devices in groups A, B, and C? I will argue that the attribution of degrees of consciousness is justified insofar as one can anticipate the filling in of a continuum from the partially functioning device at issue toward the end of the continuum — that is, toward the Cyborg.

On the verbal question of whether to call something a rational agent by virtue of its satisfying the requirements of PAL activity without regard to its actually being conscious, I will adopt the convention of allowing a candidate for consciousness that does satisfy the requirements of PAL testing (i.e., that is a pure interagency attributive language-learning and -using and independent purpose holding creature) to be called a 'rational agent'. I hope it is clear that this usage does not beg any of the substantive questions, since on this usage the question whether some device that satisfies PAL constraints is really conscious or merely appears to be conscious can be rephrased as the question whether such and such a rational agent is really conscious or merely appears to be conscious. Determining that something satisfies the requirements of PAL testing, then, will suffice to determine that the device is to some degree a rational agent, but determining that the device is to whatever degree a rational agent will not suffice to determine whether it is deserving of moral attitudes or the bearing of legal rights, or whether it experiences *qualia*.

Of course, there are some for whom the determination that something is a rational agent analytically implies the determination that it is a conscious or fully intentional system. This implication might have two sources: 1. For some, the criteria for consciousness attribution will already have come into play before a determination that something is a rational agent is made. 2. For others — logical behaviorists of late Wittgensteinian or Rylean persuasion — there can be nothing to consciousness attribution other than the determination of rational agency along behavioral and dispositional lines. The issue with the latter group is more than a merely verbal one. On this score, I take it that the other-minds question is a meaningful one; that the various *qualia* objections to logical behaviorism have force; and that there are practical epistemological questions specific to consciousness attribution to artificial devices. (For more on this, see "the blindsight argument" below.) In any case, strategically speaking, we can only benefit by attempting to come by our consciousness attribution to Cyborgs or PALs by means other than the springboard of logical behaviorism. For we wish consciousness attribution to Cyborgs to be persuasive to a wider group than logical behaviorists.

The issue between the position developed here and that of the former group, however, is more strictly verbal. I take it that such phenomena as automatism, blindsight, trance, and subconscious creation of semantic structures (e.g., poems), justify the verbal intuition allowing for a behavioral and dispositional criterion of attribution of rational agency, which leaves open the question whether the device that satisfies such a criterion is really conscious or not.

6

Does the 'Formal' Versus the 'Physical' Axis Matter?

I will begin by asking whether consciousness attribution is different for formal entities with whom one interacts through a monitor representation of an environment than for physically realized devices. Some might hold that a formal PAL even of the most elaborate kind would not be conscious simply because it is a merely formal entity. One might say that *there is nothing there to be conscious*. Gertrude Stein is supposed to have said about Los Angeles (or was it merely Oakland?) that there's "no there there." The view we're now considering about PAL is that there's "no it there."

Something like this view is found in Fodor (1982b pp. 231-233) and in Searle (1984, Chapter 2). However, several aspects of the relationship between formal representation and material embodiment are conflated in these analyses, and I hope they may be brought out by considerations of the ontological status of a PAL. Since neither Fodor nor Searle (nor, for that matter, Dennett [1978b], nor Lem's science fiction accounts [1974, 1978], nor Block's thought experimental creatures [1981]) call attention to the possibility of a formal entity interacting with a human via an input device leading to a representative agent in the formal entity's microworld, I can't say that the views we'll be examining now are *the ones* advanced by Fodor and Searle. Rather, we'll consider the matter on its merits and return afterward to an analysis of the points made by Fodor and Searle in turn.

The question, then, is 'Is there any *it* there?' I'll attempt to show that if there's no *it* there, then perhaps there's no *it* here either. Microworld PALs, I'll argue, constitute twentieth century hybrids — beings we've never before had the technological base to be able to conceive and puzzle about, let alone design and build. But although their ontological status is hybrid in a fresh and unprecedented way, the philosophical problems raised by PALs are the very old ones about universals and particulars, materiality and representation. The availability of a technology to build formal entities with whom we can interact in the interagency manner reinforces the questions Plato raised about spatiotemporal entities. But as there is no fixed contrast between the sort of thing a PAL in a formal environment is, on the one hand, and the sort of thing a person is in our world, on the other, one is not able to maintain the view that a PAL cannot be a moral agent or a conscious being because it's not enough of a thing to be anything at all.

What World Does a PAL Live In?

We'll now explore the various points of contact between the formal world of PAL and our world. My intention will be to show that even if we do not construct a real world android, but merely a formal one, we cannot dismiss considerations of its moral standing and its consciousness.

Consider a routine set of events. PAL has not eaten for a while. After consulting its maps, it finds that there is no food and that there are food seeds near Agent-2. PAL goes to the fertile area and instructs Agent-2 to bring the seeds. Now we can say that there is a specific moment at which PAL begins searching for food, a moment at which it sees food or squares off with the other agent in the environment and captures the communication floor, and so on. In order to be able to instruct Agent-2 to bring food or the seeds, it had to learn a common language with Agent-2, and this learning took place at various specific points in time. And this temporal order within which PAL lives is clearly our temporal order. If PAL acquires a certain belief or ability on March 5, 1987, this is our March 5, 1987 as well.

But what about location? We can easily say where some representation of PAL is located. There will be a screen or a number of screens on which representations of PAL can be found. But the location of PAL is not to be identified with any of these representations' locations. Similarly, we can't say how big PAL is; we can only say how big PAL is relative to something else in PAL's world. Of course, any representation of PAL will have size: On one screen PAL's image takes up two inches; on another, five inches. But we can no more answer the absolute question, 'How big is PAL?' than we can say where PAL is with reference to our spatial order.

Now we are familiar with objects that exist in a spatio-temporal order other than ours. Alice in Wonderland, and Wonderland itself, cannot be located with reference to our space. And although we are not always clear about how to think of fictional entities such as Lewis Carroll's Alice or the croquet balls she strikes, we take for granted the notion that inquiries about Alice's consciousness or her legal and moral rights are out of the question. No harm can come to Alice because she is fictional. We can change her story, but then we wouldn't really change Lewis Carroll's Alice at all: We would merely be telling another story that has some similarities with Lewis Carroll's. Even Carroll can write one draft of it, change it around and write another, and we can think of the second draft as 'the story', or we can think of there having been two stories. None of the philosophical issues surrounding the identification of fictional particulars and their ontological standing are seen as having any bearing on cognitive science or the philosophy of mind. They are seen as issues of metaphysics having no bearing on the theory of consciousness, and, indeed, this division of the territory is apt.

There is, however, a crucial difference between the ontological status of Alice and that of PAL. To begin with, although the spatial order in which Alice moves resembles the spatial order in which PAL moves, given that neither spatial order has any point of contact with our spatial order (except through being representable in it), the same is not true for the temporal order. Alice lives in a historical frame, none of whose moments can be identified with any moment in the life of the world. Even if the characters wear Victorian costumes, and even if a supposed year is given, we wouldn't say that Alice lived ninety-five years ago or whatever; we would say she is supposed to have lived ninety-five years ago. We are thus invited to contemplate a world history just like ours, except that in the time corresponding to ninety-five years ago there was an Alice to whom various interesting things happened.

However, PAL, as we've seen, lives in our temporal order. It is on September 11, 1985, say, that PAL learns how seeds make food appear; and this is the very September 11, 1985, on which day Piet Botha of South Africa warns the United States and the Soviet Union not to meddle in the internal affairs of South Africa. PAL shares our temporal order. Fictional characters such as Alice do not.

This is not a trivial difference. We participate in PAL's life in a way utterly unlike our involvement with noninteractive fictional characters. As noted, we can't make out a difference between changing Alice's story and inventing a second story that is similar in many respects to the first. There is no equivalent with PAL. PAL has a single life-history, just as any human has. No one can change PAL's life history by interacting with PAL differently, because the past interaction has taken place, is part of PAL's memory, and so on. We can, of course, take the identical PAL starting program and have people interacting with that in different places in different ways. But that is like starting with two clone-identical humans and raising them in different places, which of course is different from contemplating two different versions of a single Alice story or two somewhat similar Alice stories. The crucial feature of our relationship with a PAL creature is its interactive character. It is people — living, breathing humans — who not only teach PAL a language but also teach PAL how to accomplish various tasks based on that language. Whatever world PAL lives in, we can participate in that world, and indeed our temporal order *is* Pal's temporal order.

The puzzle, then, is that we can personally interact with a being that lives in our time but not in our space. And this feature of our relationship with a PAL, when one is built, will make for an unprecedented encounter. This ontological situation has been discussed in the context of the purported interaction between God or some personal gods and the human world. According to religious accounts of the Western world, God can intervene in human history and act upon our space, but He lives in a transcendent world outside of our space and time. We don't want to push this parallel too far though. Theologians do not place on an equal footing the world of the transcendent God with the fictional space-time of Alice in Wonderland. But we do equate the space in which PAL lives with the fictional space or sort of fictional space in which Alice lives, whereas PAL shares our temporal order with us.

In any case, the crucial distinguishing feature of our relationship with PAL as compared to our relationship with fictional characters is the interactive aspect of the former. But we now have a wholly different set of questions to ask about our relationship with entities that inhabit purely formal spaces. Because PAL begins life at a certain point in our time and dies at a certain point in our time, and because PAL's death might be caused (deliberately or inadvertently) by something a human does, it is difficult for us to avoid asking whether it is a morally indifferent thing to deliberately kill a personal agent that (who) inhabits a purely formal space.

Surely the popular initial response to such a question would be to say something like this: The only moral considerations we have in our interactions with PAL are those pertinent to the various humans who have involvement: our obligations to the people who designed PAL (we must not spoil the one good copy of the program, for instance); our obligations to the people who have instructed PAL (we mustn't waste their efforts by killing PAL if killing PAL means that PAL's memories are unretrievable, particularly if they want to continue with further instruction in order to study the program better); our obligations to the scientific community in general (we mustn't detract from scientific research by wantonly killing PAL). But, one would continue along these lines, we have no obligations whatsoever to PAL; PAL bears no rights at all, since it inhabits a merely formal spatial order. The fact that we share PAL's temporal space is totally irrelevant, one would go on to say. It's absurd to think that one would have an obligation to a purely formal entity, even if it interacts with us in our time, since we cannot point to the space in which it lives. It has no body. How can we inflict pain or suffering on an entity that has a merely formal body? The very notion of inflicting pain on a formal entity, a bodiless body, is an absurdity, a laughable folly that only some deluded philosopher might consider with any degree of seriousness.

This seems so obviously to be the case that some time must be spent stoking the fire of the opposite viewpoint. So let's do that. On the assumption that all and only persons bear moral rights, we can use this question as a test of the attributability of consciousness, or personhood, to PAL.

Perhaps the easiest way of showing that formal entities, or entities whose bodies inhabit merely formal spaces, might be conscious is to construct a variant of the brain in a vat hypothesis. Suppose some fellow's brain is extracted and kept alive in a vat that supplies oxygen to it; suppose further that the brain, through the discoveries of future science, is hooked up to a set of interpreters that transmit messages to a computer hooked up to a monitor with which a human can interact by operating an Agent-2 element. Model perceptual information is also fed back to the interpreters and passed on to the brain in the vat. Thus we have a real human brain operating and interacting with human beings in real human time. The physical brain occupies space in our spatial order, just as the floppy disk containing the PAL program occupies space in our spatial order. But the environment in which the body, so to speak, which the brain gives messages to, is a purely formal environment and is "merely represented" to us for the purposes of our being able to interact with this entity which has a merely formal body connected with an actual brain.

The person whose doings are created by that brain we can call Mr. Blank. Blank's ontological status is a great conundrum: he has a life history, learns a language, narrowly avoids being wiped out by some threat, remembers certain things and not others, talks to people — actual people — and thus becomes part of the life history of every actual human person he interacts with. Blank perceives objects, has beliefs, and, at a certain point, ceases to exist, presumably having had one too many brushes with danger, for example, or having been put out of existence by a human deliberately or accidentally, or having been unable to get food in time to ward off extinction through starvation. (An environment program connected to the vat cuts off oxygen to the brain under the appropriate circumstances.)

Yet, when we ask where Mr. Blank is at any moment during which Blank is a functioning cognitive system, we cannot locate Blank's body. Blank inhabits a formal world whose locations have no point of contact with our world. Blank's brain is, of course, the one exception to this, because it is in some sense part of Blank's body, or part of Blank at any rate. And Blank's brain is not only locatable in our world but is actually a human brain.

Yet, despite the weirdness of the arrangement, most people would probably be tempted to say that the brain in the vat is conscious. The fact that its doings go on in a merely formal space would not prevent the attribution of consciousness to Mr. Blank. Thus, the initial intuition that an entity with a merely formal body cannot be conscious is not nearly as secure as it first appears. The moral that one can draw from the story of Mr. Blank is that the burden of consciousness attribution falls on the nature of the embodiment of the information processor more than on anything else.

This lesson is only further bolstered by consideration of the arbitrariness of what is to be regarded an actual physical body and what is to be regarded a merely formal body inhabiting a formal space. Imagine, for example, that we have a lab in which an environment is created as a three-dimensional (3-D) equivalent of PAL's formal environment. Then there will be an actual robot whose functioning is a physical, three-dimensional, interpretation of the formal structure we give to PAL. PAL, the 3-D robot, has a grasper, a sensor, a locomotor, and so on. And the functioning of this 3-D robot is a direct interpretation of the capacities of PAL as a formal entity. The floppy disk with the cognitive program remains unchanged, although it is now inside a moving robot. And perhaps PAL's instructor will teach via a remote connection with an actual 3-D Agent-2 compubot that functions in the artificial environment lab. So it may not be all that easy to say whether the Agent-2 compubot is to be regarded as Agent-2's body. But it will be easy to identify the location of PAL's body. Under such a set-up, PAL will share not only our temporal order but also our spatial order.

Once again, the dismissal of the possibility that PAL is conscious or has moral status based on its bodilessness seems insecure. The floppy disk is the same both in the original case and in the instantiated-in-our-world case; in the former case, it's connected to a set of monitors that represent; in the latter, it's connected (or inside) a compubot that moves about in a room in our world. There seems to be no good principle available with which one can distinguish the moral possibilities of the one case from the purported moral irrelevancy of the other.

But we can go further than this. What if we have a single floppy disk computer unit that is connected to four or five or ten rooms, each set up in a functionally identical way and each containing a compubot that interprets the motor output of the cognitive processor. In each of these rooms, we may imagine, there is also a 3-D robot connected to a single unit that receives the input given by PAL's human instructor.

Now we can no longer easily identify the location of PAL. Moreover, each compubot that receives PAL's message seems, for all intents and purposes, to be a representation, or an interpretation, of a formal entity — a PAL that has mere formal status as an object. The distinction between things that have formal status only and those that are given to us as mere representations, on the one hand, and things that are objects in the world, on the other hand, no longer seems at all secure. Something is not said to be a representation simply by virtue of its having only two dimensions instead of three; a sculpture can be as much a representation as a painting. When PAL's cognitive program is hooked up to a single compubot, should we regard the robot hardware plus computer as the object-in-the-world that is PAL? Or should we regard the hardware as a moving 3-D sculptural representation of a formal order whose cognitive program is materially implicated in a particular piece of computer hardware — namely, a particular floppy disk? It seems impossible to give any grounds for preferring one over the other.

There are still other set-ups to contemplate: Say we take a few PALs and have them inhabit the same environment. The human-operated agent teaches both PALs to talk, and they start communicating with each other. The human-operated agent withdraws from the scene. Now we have two PALs talking to each other, seeing each other, and so on. Do they still inhabit our time? Imagine that we now speed up the computer reaction-processing times so that the whole life story of these PALs happens within a few moments. In some sense they still inhabit our time. But imagine that another level of the program records all the representations, decisions, and even quasi-arbitrary calculations that are built into PAL's system of cognition. Then we can replay the life stories of these PALs.

While it's true that only the original events constituted the making of the decisions, the quasi-arbitrary algorithms have been generated in ways that are, in principle, predictable. Can't we regard the original making of the decision in our time as being merely a representation of a life story that was entirely predictable in principle, hence merely a representation of a life story or a set of life stories in our time? In the same way, the later replays are representations of the same life story at later points in our time. The formal world occupied by these PALs, then, is not only spatial but temporal. The Platonist conclusions about space, time, and matter as representative of a timeless formal order become increasingly inescapable. And the more we see our own lives as conceivably predictable in principle, the more necessary it is that we grapple again with these ancient questions.

The implications of all these cases is that even if we do not build a real-world robotic implementation of the model android — in other words, even if we do not move past the second of our android construction steps — we cannot dismiss consideration of the sentience of the entity. The distinction between having a body and having a representation of a body is not a sharp one. In the variations we have been considering we cannot say which entities are *merely formal* and which are not; or, at least, we cannot base such judgments on any perspicuous principles. We cannot, then, avoid considering the sentience of a formal android on the grounds that it lacks a body.

Let's turn now to other arguments which hold that something can't be a mind because it is a mere formalism. First, we'll look briefly at Fodor's (1982b) view that a device such as Terry Winograd's SHRDLU has access only to formal or nonsemantic properties of the representations it manipulates and, therefore, cannot attribute meanings to its representations. We'll then turn to a more detailed look at Searle's view (1982, 1984) on the relationship between formal representations and the material properties of embodiments of them.

Fodor rightly calls to our attention the fact that SHRDLU cannot be taken to be making statements about anything. There are two reasons for this, according to Fodor, although he does not clearly separate them. One is that the microworld is merely formal; there are no cubes and blocks to be talking about. As he puts it, SHRDLU is a computer dreaming it's a robot. The second reason is that its statements are not being made by a semantic user, as it might be termed; we humans are the ones who are attributing the meanings to the representations put out by the system. The machine has no access to the interpretations of its representations; therefore, it is not making any statements about anything. So it is not making statements.

Now the latter point has to do with the specific limitations of SHRDLU as a system. SHRDLU is not a pure or perception-based system; it is not, as I've argued above, a candidate for rational agent because it doesn't identify its human interlocutor as an agent in its environment. Moreover, there is no evidence that it has independent purposes; it doesn't have any such. The second point raised by Fodor, then, need not be true of all formal systems. SHRDLU has no access to the interpretations of its representations, but some other perception-based system might. Indeed, if SHRDLU were given a real-world embodiment robot in a lab with blocks and cubes and pyramids, the bare point that SHRDLU has no access to the interpretations of its representations would not be true. It wouldn't be dreaming that it was a robot. It would be a robot. But it wouldn't therefore be a language-using robot. Over and above access to interpretation issues, then, is the nature of the functioning of a rational agent as a holder of independent purposes and as an entity capable of functioning in the interagency attributive manner. And SHRDLU would not pass those tests. Fodor's second point is thus addressed by the design of a PAL.

Fodor's first point is addressed by the sorts of considerations adduced above concerning the shakiness of our intuition about what a mere representation is as opposed to an actual embodiment. Fodor seems to have gotten tangled up in the assumption that far more sophisticated conceptions than SHRDLU are not available to us. If his conclusions are meant to apply to impure (or non-perception-based) systems only, they stand. But if they are meant to apply more generally, his analysis collapses. And it does seem that he wants to draw sweeping conclusions: He suggests that it is the computational theory of the mind that is the source of the gap between a language user and a device such as SHRDLU. But as we've seen, this conclusion is not justified. People working on machine simulations with linguistic representation may not have succeeded in constructing semantic systems, but there is nothing in Fodor's analysis that addresses the question of whether such a task is legitimate. As I've tried to show, it is a proper research goal to attempt to specify the computational mechanisms whereby an embodying system is a language-*using* device; in addition, we are now able to start working in a practical way on designing and constructing such an integrated system. Of course this leaves open the question of whether a system that *appears* to meet the *behavioral* criteria of being a rational agent (or meets the behavioral criteria and therefore appears to be a rational agent) must *be* a truly conscious device. But as should now be clear, no hand-waving about something's being a 'mere formalism' will solve this problem. Once we see that (1) integrated system design is available to us and that (2) there is no fixed demarcation between a 'merely formal' instantiation of an integrated system and an 'actual embodiment' of an integrated system, we'll recognize that we have as yet seen no grounds to conclude from something's being a formal system that it cannot, therefore, be a language-using system. Either it will turn out that there are sufficient grounds from behavioral criteria

7

Do We Need to Peek
to Attribute Consciousness?

Searle's main concern is to remind us that consciousness is implicated in a particular way with materiality. Something that is not implicated with materiality in this way cannot be conscious; it cannot have mind. And since, he says, a computer program is defined by its formal properties, whereas intentional states are about the things of the world, something will not have mind merely by virtue of instantiating a computer program (Searle 1984, Chapter 2). Moreover, for something to have mind, it will have to embody its formalisms in a particular kind of materiality. Its material embodiment must have causal powers at least equivalent to the causal powers of the human brain.

Now Searle has been roundly criticized for the apparent vacuousness of his analysis. On the one hand, he is clearly willing to grant that some inorganic matter *might* have the right sort of causal powers to cause mind. On the other hand, he gives no analysis whatever of the way we are to discover whether some embodiment of a formal system is or is not the right sort to cause mind. Zenon Pylyshyn (1980), for example, imagines a gradual substitution of integrated circuit chips for brain cells. According to Searle, it's conceivable that at the outset the person who had the organic brain was making a statement; but by the time the substitution was completed, the system producing the sounds was no longer an intentional system. It is only the (presumably human) listener who now attributes meanings to the sounds, and not the system that produces the sounds. But on what basis can we tell whether a particular embodiment is or is not the right sort? Since Searle gives no answer to this question, the theory appears to be vacuous. And some form of functionalism that holds the type of material embodiment to be irrelevant seems to be the only option.

I would now like to suggest that if we are to assess the debate between Searle and his critics, we must keep clear about three distinct axes of interest:

1. Formal representation versus material embodiment
2. The material type of a particular embodiment
3. Behavioral criteria of agency attribution versus the combination of behavioral criteria and means of material embodiment criteria for agency attribution, or attribution of mentality or consciousness

Searle's conflation of these distinct axes of interest has made it too easy for his critics to demolish his analysis. Or, to put it another way, Searle's critics have fallen into the traps of Searle's confusions and have thus been led to a much too easy functionalist epistemology — namely, the version which holds that it is exclusively by virtue of the proper functionally described behavior a thing engages in, or is capable of engaging in, that something is properly judged to be an intentional system, or a system that has mind.

Searle appears to be trading pretty much exclusively in (1), the issue of formal representation versus actual material embodiment, when he says that for a system to have mind it must not only exhibit the functional design or organization of an undoubtedly conscious system, but must also be instantiated in a physical system of the same sort, or in one with similar powers, because otherwise it might be a mere simulation. As he puts it, "no one supposes that a computer simulation of a storm will leave us all wet, or a computer simulation of a fire is likely to burn the house down. Why on earth would anyone in his right mind suppose a computer simulation of mental processes actually had mental processes? I don't really know the answer to that, since the idea seems to me, to put it frankly, quite crazy from the start" (Searle 1984, p. 38). Searle is relying here on the idea that a formal representation of something will not be a material embodiment of it: His argument thus trades on the first axis of interest.

On this score, Searle's critics are right. No one would disagree with the idea that from system S being a formal representation of system T, it does not follow that S is itself a T. The assent to that, however, does not imply that S is not a T. By itself, the analogy with computer simulations of the weather is unpersuasive, or question begging. To see this, we can consider a different simulation — a simulation not of the weather or a fire but of a clock. Outside some building is a sundial. Inside the building is a computer with a model of the functioning of the sundial outside the building: The rising and setting of the model sun has been synchronized with the rising and setting of the sun as observed from the site of the sundial outside the building. Now it would be appropriate to quip, "We don't expect a computer simulation of the weather to get us wet, so why should we expect a computer simulation of a sundial to *be* a sundial, or to indicate time off the light of the sun?" But it would not be appropriate to quip, "We don't expect a computer simulation of the weather to get us wet, so why should we expect a computer simulation of a sundial to be a clock?" The computer simulation of the sundial outside the building would be every bit as good a clock, an indicator of time, as the sundial itself.

The question is whether the relation of consciousness to the brain is more like the relation of water to a storm or the relation of a clock to a sundial. It *is* a crazy idea to expect a computer simulation of a human being to *be* a human being; but just as a computer simulation of a sundial might itself be a clock, so a computer simulation of a human being might itself *be* one of the things a human being is — namely, conscious.

Searle does not rest his case on the meteorology analogy alone, however. He also asks us to consider the shuffling cards analogy (derived from Block 1978). Against functionalists who would suggest that a computerized robot, if given the appropriate program, would be conscious, Searle objects that the same program could be functionally instantiated by a vast number of people each holding some card or other, and told under what circumstances to trade the card to some neighbor. Imagine, the objection continues, billions of these people making their trades, shuffling cards among themselves in accordance with the complex program. How absurd it would be if we had to say that the corporate being suddenly becomes conscious merely by virtue of the isomorphy between the program it (the corporate being) instantiates and the structure of the cognition of the human. How absurd to think that the conglomerate thing, made up of billions of people, constitutes a unified conscious entity.

Our intuitions are strained somewhat by the effort to conceive of this conglomerate entity as conscious —partly, what strains our intuitions is the vast scale, the apparent non-entityness of the entity since it consists mostly of space between the people shuffling their cards around, and so on.

But this intuition test really is deceptive. First of all, there is a perspective from which we humans can be considered incredibly vast conglomerate entities within whom is mostly empty space, despite the enormous number of atoms in our bodies. From that microperspective, we are corporate beings no more compact than the vast conglomerate being made of people shuffling cards around. Envisioned from the microperspective, it makes no sense to imagine us as integrated unified beings with consciousness. And yet we are.

Second, if these vast conglomerate beings are proper instantiations of a cognitive structure isomorphic with the structure of human cognition, then there ought really to be some envisionable perspective from which the idea that the conglomerate being is conscious becomes not so counterintuitive. Imagine, for example, that while travelling to some distant outpost in space, we approach a planet that we know to be vast in scale compared to earth; and from millions of miles away, we see creatures evidently relating to each other in apparently intelligent fashion, as intentional beings. Seen from this perspective, millions of miles away, they appear to be beings organized into trunks, limbs, eyes, speech organs, and so on. Then as we come close, we lose sight of that perspective because we can see only bits and pieces on so small a scale that it no longer is apparent how the entity — now seen as a conglomerate, a corporate entity — can constitute a single, integrated, conscious being. In this example, though, once we've had the experience of being able to see the beings from the right perspective, we wouldn't be so likely to find the scale a permanent obstacle to our holding these creatures to be conscious beings. Searle's argument is a form of faulty scalism. (For similar criticisms, see Lycan 1981. Note also that other problematic cases presented by Block [1978, 1981] either fall prey to similar criticisms or fail to get off the ground once purity and other PAL requirements are checked for.)

In both cases, then, Searle has relied on our intuitions that something might be a mere simulation or a mere formal representation as opposed to an 'actual embodiment' of a functioning consciousness. Counteranalogies such as those of the sundial or the hypothetical material substitution that Pylyshyn presents, succeed in undermining reliance on these intuitions — but specifically by jumping forward to the substantial challenge to produce the principle according to which material embodiment or means of material instantiation might be relevant to the determination of the intentionality of a system. This obscures the point that the demolition of Searle's analysis is due to the success of the argument against the clarity of a general distinction between mere simulation or mere formal representation and actual embodiment. As we've seen in some detail, there is no such clear distinction to apply to an integrated system that includes an interagency attributive PAL. Searle's argument thus fails: A supposed distinction between simulation and actual embodiment cannot be used to establish the relevance of the type of material embodiment for proper attribution of consciousness.

But it does not follow that the material type of an embodiment is not relevant; nor does it follow that the way some matter embodies formalism is not relevant to the determination of whether it has mind. This brings us to a consideration of axes (2) and (3).

Our strategy here will be to compare a certain paradigmatic Cyborg to a human. Assume that we have a computer inside an otherwise empty skull, and that the computer is appropriately hooked up to the rest of the normal human body. We are not interested in what happened to the original brain or person or 'self' of the human prior to the transplant. If we need to tell a full story, it will be that an infant experienced brain death, but not heart death, and an artificial brain was transplanted into its skull. The artificial brain or computer has the structure of a newborn human brain, and the baby was subsequently raised and became an adult. Assume that there is no way of knowing whether an apparent human is a Cyborg of this kind or not, except by peeking inside the skull by means of X-rays, by operating, or by being told by someone who had seen the computer in the skull by means of X-rays or had witnessed an operation, and so on. In this discussion we'll refer to such an entity as a 'Cyborg'.

Our question, now, is this: Is a Cyborg conscious? Could there be any reason to think that a human is conscious but a Cyborg is not? It is in answer to this question that the distinction appears between (2), the type of material embodiment, and (3), the means whereby some matter embodies form.

Searle seems to be claiming that the type of material embodiment is relevant since the material embodiment of some program has to have the causal powers that yield a conscious system. Presumably, then, the type of materiality counts: Some types of material embodiment might have the right sort of causal powers, whereas others would not. However, when we search Searle for a specification of the principle whereby type of materiality is relevant, we find nothing. And it is hard to think of what specifically might enable us to say that the material embodiment A of program P is conscious but the material embodiment B of the same program P is not conscious. As Searle puts it, "Suppose that Martians arrived on earth and we concluded that they had mental states. But suppose that when their heads were opened up, it was discovered that all they had inside was green slime. Well still, the green slime . . . would have to have causal powers equal to those of the human brain" (Searle 1984, p. 41). Here Searle has neatly undone himself, for if we can determine that Martians have minds without peeking inside their skulls, then it can hardly matter what we discover inside their skulls, and the type of material embodiment is not relevant to something's being conscious or not. Nor can there be any correspondence

between material type and observable behavior discovered empirically, since the question at issue is whether anything that exhibited
similar behavior would be conscious or have mind. Once again, Searle's
analysis collapses for lack of a principle that will distinguish the right
sort of embodiment of a program from the wrong sort of embodiment
of a program.

It is at this point, however, that the conflation of axes (2) and (3) must
be avoided. We cannot conclude that the irrelevance of the type of
material that accomplishes the embodiment of a program implies that
the way a program is embodied in a material system is irrelevant. To put
this more generally, it may be that material M embodied in a functional
system C is not conscious, but that the same material M causing
behavior that is externally indistinguishable from that of the first
system and is embodied in means of embodiment D is conscious.
Functionally described behavior alone, then, would not be sufficient to
determine whether something is conscious; and although the argument
Searle presents has been demolished, his main conclusion would still
stand.

Of course, if this distinction between type of material and type of
causal embodiment is to have any content, some positive account must
be given of how there might be relevantly different means of embodying a set of functional relations. I will consider two such accounts.

The Blindsight Argument

Consider the following argument based on some overly neat but conceptually useful speculations concerning the phenomenon known as
'blindsight'. Blindsight is the ability to use information coming through
the eyes without experiencing the source of the information as sight. It
occurs in some people after damage to the visual cortex (Churchland
1986, pp. 224-227).

Now suppose that we discover that in humans, visual information is
sorted out in two parallel paths, A and B. When the B pathway is broken,
there is no conscious awareness of seeing. But if the A pathway is un-
impeded, some of the visual information will still be available to the
person, who will nevertheless not have the experience of seeing. Suppose, as well, that the B pathway exhibits some distinctive physico-
functional features; that there are A and B pathways for learning, taste,
smell, touch, and thought processes; and that the distinctive features of
organization of the visual B pathway are present in all the B pathways
but nowhere else. These suppositions present us with as strong a case

as we have thus far seen for the Searlian who argues that consciousness is produced only in structuro-functional embodiments of a certain type. The hypothesis would be that the common features of the B routes are the features that produce or are required for consciousness. We will call these features the CA (consciousness-associated) features.

The question that arises is this: Can CA features be created in material other than that which composes the B pathways of the human brain? Are they merely being simulated when similar systems of organization using other materials are being employed?

Since the hypothesis that CA features are not merely associated with consciousness but are causally related to the occurrence of the consciousness emerged from an empirical test of the dissociability of consciousness from informational content, it is reasonable to suppose that one might want to match such empirical dissociability in the Cyborg. That is, one might want to ensure that the Cyborg was at least subject to the same abnormal functioning as the human — in other words, that there were buildable Cyborgs who (that) processed information in parallel paths and, when the B pathways were cut, would report no experience of seeing, tasting, and so on, but nevertheless could make judgments showing that all or some of the information was available to them.

There are two cases to consider then: (1) We can build a Cyborg that appears to have the same type of blindsight, 'deafaudition', and so forth, as the human when the B pathways are cut. And (2), although we can build devices that pass the normal Cyborg test — that is, no one can tell who is or isn't a Cyborg except by consulting hospital records, taking X-rays of the skull and the like — try as we may, we can't build a Cyborg whose abnormal functioning works this way. We create what appears to be simulation of the double pathway structure, yet when we cut pathway B, either there remains the report of conscious experience of the matter at hand, or there is neither conscious experience of the matter at hand nor any surviving information available to the Cyborg.

Obviously, these cases as described are rather neat and simplistic. But if we can't construct a proper blindsight argument from the neat and simple cases, then we are very far indeed from having a sound argument from the blindsight-like cases, and, in general, far from having a sound argument showing how structuro-functional means of material embodiment can be relevant to the identification of true consciousnesses as opposed to merely simulated consciousnesses.

Let's consider the two cases in turn.

(1) We have a Cyborg who manifests blindsight and other apercep-

tual behavior when the B pathways are cut. What possible grounds could we now have to attribute true consciousness, true experience of *qualia* and so on, to the human but not to the artificial device? The Searlian might worry that the causal powers sufficient for the production of consciousness are not there in the other stuff. But once again, the worry is a programmatic piece of metaphysics that is not rooted in any epistemological praxis with regard to consciousness attribution to the device in question. That the functional elements of the CA features have been reproduced in the Cyborg is guaranteed *ex hypothesi*. But if there can be a genuine worry about whether the Cyborg is really conscious at all, despite the functional reproduction of the paired pathways (one with the features and the other with the non-CA features) then — if such devices are ever built — the world will have an insoluable ethico-epistemological dilemma posed by an unanswerable metaphysical question.

It is useful to note that this problem does not occur in the case of consciousness attribution to other humans. To be sure, there is, or may be, a rootless metaphysical doubt about the true consciousness of other humans. The solipsist within many of us can at least find meaningful the basic other-minds question: 'But what if I am the only true consciousness?' If the Wittgensteinian, or Rylean, logical behaviorist does not succeed in demolishing the notion that the inverted spectrum hypothesis, or the attribution of true experience of *qualia* over and above behavioral dispositions, are meaningful hypotheses, then at least we will find the metaphysical doubt concerning other minds answered by some version of the argument by analogy. The physico-functional makeup of other humans is *so much* like mine that it seems perverse to seriously question whether they have genuine experience at all. But it is precisely the conjunction of the physical and the functional that is being separated by the Cyborg case. The argument by analogy trades both on material analogy and analogy of functional organization with consciousness attribution to other humans. The case of the Cyborg compels us to assess the functional analogy without a complete physical analogy. And we seem to lack the tools to construct a scale with which to make such an assessment. The Searlian, perhaps, will point to the attribution of consciousness to other humans hoping to elicit the intuition that the physical part of the analogy was decisive or at least an important element in the analogy. The functionalist simply does not have that intuition. 'What does it matter what my matter is?' intuits the functionalist, who then denies that the material analogy was ever of much relevance. Hence the hope for an analytic solution appears to be at a dead end: The Searlian voice has not quite been answered.

But this is not the end of the analysis. For although the metaphysical dialectic may have reached a dead end, the essence of the other-minds problem, whether in the case of human-to-human attribution or human-to-Cyborg attribution, will turn on the intertwining of at least epistemological and metaphysical concerns. ('At least' because moral concerns may need to be entered too as we'll shortly see.) The purely metaphysical other-minds problem in the human-to-human case is resolved by the recognition that there is a practical principle or criterion provided by the physico-functional analogy. To see that the Searlian query 'But what if the material isn't sufficient to produce true consciousness, despite all the functional similarity?' is as arbitrary as the question 'But what if I'm the only real consciousness despite my behavioral and physical similarities to other humans?' we need only consider that the Searlian must grant that some other material than the human material with the appropriate organization *might* have the causal powers sufficient to produce consciousness. It is the Searlian who has no adequate *practical* response to the simple question of identifying, making intelligible, or accounting for, in any way, why some kind of material does have the requisite causal powers and the other doesn't. A rough analogy is the solipsist who, of necessity, has no practical way to deal with his own concession that other humans *might have* consciousness, but refuses to take physico-functional similarity as an adequate criterion or ground for identifying the apparently conscious behavior that is accompanied by true consciousness from that which is not. The Searlian, like the solipsist, *might* say, 'But what if the world isn't fundamentally rational on this point?' Yet that, surely, is sufficient to establish the superiority of the functionalist approach. This approach makes sense of the situation in practical terms in a way that the Searlian has thus far, in principle, been unable to do.

In addition, one might want to mention the moral argument, which proceeds as follows: If the Cyborg is truly sentient and we do not grant it sentient status, we have made a terrible moral error. If the Cyborg is truly sentient and we do grant it sentient status, we have behaved properly. If the Cyborg is not truly sentient and we grant it sentient status we have not committed any moral offense. We have simply been acting politely to a stone, as it were. And if it is not truly sentient and we do not grant it sentient status, we have not committed any moral offense. The only high moral stake is found in the case of its being sentient. *Other considerations being equal*, this argument is surely in favor of liberalism rather than chauvinism in consciousness attribution. And as we've just seen, for the Searlian other things are equal, for the Searlian finds the situation fundamentally puzzling and lacks any principle by which to distinguish the right sort of matter from the wrong sort. The functionalist assumes that nature is not fundamentally arbitrary or unintelligible on this score and has reason to attribute consciousness to the Cyborg even before the moral stakes are considered.

On two grounds, then, the functionalist position is superior to the Searlian position. It should be stressed here that it is the epistemic consideration, the assumption of fundamental intelligibility, that is the decisive issue. The moral consideration is a practical one and does not address the question quite at the level at which it has been raised. Like Pascal's argument, which at best tells us nothing about God's existence but only about how we ought to behave, the moral argument does not address the question whether the Cyborg has true experience, it addresses the question as to how we ought to treat the Cyborg *in case* it does have true consciousness.

(2) What, then, of the second case? The functionalist will want to give two answers. The first is strategic. The second has to do with the coherence of the hypothesis.

The strategy that we have been following is to see whether there can be a justification for withholding the attribution of consciousness to a Cyborg based on some aspect of its structuro-functional organization that does not result in externally observable or behavioral differences from the human. In the case of the Cyborg that doesn't respond like the human when the CA pathways are blocked, we have jumped outside the boundary of our original question, for we are no longer quite dealing with a case of behavioral similarity or indistinguishability. Although the problems of consciousness attribution in cases where there is no isomorphic behavior need to be addressed, the idea was to address them *only after* an analysis of consciousness attribution in the behaviorally isomorphic situation — the latter being the conceptually simpler one to deal with. Thus we are justified in postponing considerations of this second case until after all the arguments have been canvassed for the case of the behaviorally isomorphic Cyborg. (True, some of the Cyborgs, the ones who despite the cut of the CA pathways still report conscious awareness will not be distinguishable without our knowing about the cut in the CA pathways; but the others will be. In the former case we would just be faced with in an epistemic vacuum.)

According to the hypothesis, we have apparently reproduced the functional elements of both pathways; yet we find that neither the Cyborg's reports nor the Cyborg's behavior matches the reports or behavior of the human. Either the Cyborg continues to report consciousness of the information, or the Cyborg reports no conscious awareness of visual information and, in addition, is unable to use the information in the way that the human does in such situations. The functionalist will now inquire as to the basis on which we have judged that the functional elements of both the A and B pathways have been reproduced in the Cyborg. Surely a test of our having correctly identified the functional elements of these pathways would be the similarity of the behavioral responses in a Cyborg built along the lines of the plan of the A and B pathways of the human. The functionalist, then, is sure to balk at the coherence of the hypothesis or, at the very least, at its empirical probability. Thus, the strength of the Searlian position seems to be inversely proportional to the plausibility of the thought experiment under which the Searlian conclusion would be warranted. I will now elaborate this point in more detail, constructing a highly improbable but conceptually clear case to show how far we must depart from empirical plausibility in order to fully or clearly justify the Searlian position.

Functional Preemption

The coherence of the hypothesis of a Cyborg in which functional elements had apparently been reproduced, although aperceptual phenomena were not found upon the cutting of the putative CA pathways is at best doubtful. However, some thought experimental conditions *are* coherent and, if found to be instantiated in the actual world, would justify the Searlian position.

Consider, for instance, two mechanical alarm clocks. Assume, further, that they are both made of metal of the same type, and that the mechanical construction of the two clocks is the same. Each clock has a dial that shows the minutes and the hours; and each has a hand that may be used to set the alarm. Because these clocks are mechanical devices of a rather elementary kind, it is possible in principle to examine the internal state of the gears and springs to discover what the internal alarm set is independently from the alarm set indicated on the dial.

Now let's say I have two such clocks on my night table, and I set them both, in the normal way, to go off at 6:00 A.M.: I turn the set-alarm hands to indicate 6:00 A.M. But on inspection, clock A turns out to have the internal alarm set of 8:00 A.M.: whereas clock B has external and internal alarm sets coinciding at 6:00 A.M. We would expect, then, that only clock B would ring at 6:00 A.M.

Nevertheless, it is conceivable that both clock A and clock B ring at 6:00 A.M. Indeed, it is conceivable that clock A *always* goes off in accordance or in coincidence with the external alarm set, regardless of whether the internal alarm set is connected or coincides with the external alarm set. Clock B, on the other hand, always goes off just as we'd expect it to, in accordance with the internal alarm set, regardless of whether the internal alarm set is in coincidence with the external alarm set.

What conditions would have to be met in order for clock A to go off always in accordance with the external alarm set and not the internal alarm set? First, ordinary physical regularities would have to be violated. Say clock A has an external alarm set of 6:00 A.M. and an internal alarm set of 8:00 A.M. As 6:00 A.M. approaches, certain gears should remain stationary; the spring that releases the alarm bell should remain unsprung. But lo and behold, the first gear or lever that would normally move following the pulling of the alarm trigger begins to move on its own and the subsequent gears therefore start moving as well; then the alarm goes off just as the hour hand reaches the 6:00 position. The ordinary sequences of physical cause and effect would have to be broken somewhere with the initiation of a motion that is not compatible with the causal regularities of physics as applied to this case.

Second, if we are to conceive of a clock that always goes off in accordance with its external alarm set rather than its internal alarm set, we must be able to conceive of a state of affairs in which function preempts physics. The description of the external alarm set is part of a functional description of the state of the clock as an alarm clock. The description of the internal alarm set is part of the description of the physics of this physical system (independent of its function as an alarm clock). Such goings on will not be expressible as physical regularities.

Since it is conceivable that a clock will go off in accordance with its external alarm set and not its internal alarm set, it is conceivable that we will discover with respect to some physical system that its functional organization preempts its physical organization in some specified circumstances. I will call such a system a 'functionally preemptive system'. A system whose functional outcomes are uniquely specified by the physical regularities of its components' states and those of its environment I will call a 'machine'.

Thus, if something is a machine, it will have two types of analysis: The first is a functional analysis, or a description of what it does, what it accomplishes, and what purposes it serves. The second is an analysis of the means whereby these functions or purposes are accomplished in terms of the physical regularities governing the changes of its component parts, such that the physical changes of any component B would be seen to occur regardless of local separation of the component from its immediately surrounding components.

In order to see in more detail that functionally preemptive outcomes are not expressible as the outcomes of physical regularities, consider an attempt to express the regular ringing of the alarm of a clock in accordance with its external alarm set, regardless of its internal alarm set as the outcome of an antecedent physical state. If clock A's alarm always rang in that fashion, one might come to regard the external alarm set as the physical cause of the ringing of the alarm. And so long as a single procedure existed for establishing the external alarm set, there would be some plausibility for such a view. But what response would one make if it were further discovered that upon repainting the numbers with words, say such that 'six' was painted in the spot that previously contained the numeral '7' and so on right around the dial, the alarm now rang in accordance with its new external alarm set rather than according to the time that would have been indicated following the old setting of the numerals? For example, when the external alarm set hand pointed to the new word 'six' the clock rang at six o'clock, not seven o'clock — despite the fact that the clock used to ring at seven o'clock with the external alarm set hand positioned in the same place. Obviously an infinity of referring conventions might be established and yet the ringing of the alarm would be taking place in response to the conventionally established meaning of the external alarm set rather than in response to the physical placement of the external alarm set hand.

One might object that two people could establish contradictory conventions. In one language '8' refers to the number 7, whereas in our language '8' refers to the number 8. Then if the external alarm set is pointing to '8', when would the alarm ring? The answer is that if we had a strange clock of this kind, we would set up experiments to find out what it would do. Perhaps it would ring in accordance with the external alarm set as understood by the person who set it. Perhaps it would ring in accordance with the external alarm set as understood by the majority of conscious beings who know it to be set pointing to '8'. And so on. The point is that the ringing of the alarm in response to a conventionally established referential token on the alarm set dial, rather than the physical placement of the alarm set hand and its physically associated elements, prevents one from regarding the ringing of the alarm as having been physically caused by the placement of the external alarm set hand. There is no purely physical regularity to be observed. The ringing of the alarm is occurring not as a function of the physical placement of the external alarm set hand, but as a function of the conventionally established meaning of the placement of the alarm set hand.

Now one might still try to rescue the idea that the alarm is going off in accordance with a physically identifiable cause by suggesting that it is the physical state of the brain of the being who sets the external alarm set hand that causes the ringing of the alarm at the appropriate time. In response to this, however, several points must be observed: First and foremost, we are envisioning a clock of this kind to serve as an illustration of how the brain might not be a physically mechanistic system in any ordinary sense. We cannot assume, then, that there is a state of the brain identifiable in physical terms that is the cause of the ringing of the alarm. Just as there is no way to represent the state of the external alarm set hand as an instance of a physical regularity connected with the ringing of the alarm, there might be no way to represent the state of the brain in physical terms as the cause of the ringing of the alarm. For the brain might itself be like this unusual clock, only more so: That is, it might have unusual violations of ordinary physical regularities going on within it: but unlike the clock, it might not even have any physical state corresponding to the external alarm set in the clock. (As we shall see, Eccles [1976] has already claimed that the brain is a device of this sort. His evidence, however, will be found wanting.)

Second, and in a more trivial fashion, we can conceive of a clock that rings according to some conventionally established meaning of some external alarm set even when the external alarm set has been set accidentally, and without having been seen as being so set by any sentient being. Surely in such cases, no cause would be representable as an instance of a physical regularity.

We were looking for a support to the idea that although the type of material found in the embodiment of a functional system might be irrelevant, there might be important differences in the way some embodiment accomplishes its function. And with the distinction between functionally preemptive systems and machines we have the support we were looking for. Two clocks made of the same type of metal and constructed in the same way might embody different sorts of causal systems. One might be functionally preemptive while the other is a machine. And two clocks might be made of different types of material, one metal, and the other plastic, say, and yet both accomplish their function in the same way — namely, as machines or as functionally preemptive systems, as the case may be.

Let's now apply this analysis to Cyborgs and humans. The distinction between a Cyborg and a human is the distinction between two types of material embodying a system whose functional behavior is the same in both cases of embodiment as externally measured or observed.

A human has an organic brain; a Cyborg has a computer in the place of a human's brain. But we can't tell from the behavior of a putative human whether it is a Cyborg or not. Now the challenge issued was to find a principle that would justify peeking in the attribution of consciousness once PAL and all behavioral requirements had been checked for. The hard line functionalist finds no possible ground in the mere type of material to justify attributing consciousness or mind to a system in one case and withholding the attribution in another case. In this the functionalist is justified. But aside from the issue of material type is the type of causal system the material embodies; and just as we can imagine functionally preemptive causal systems in the case of clocks, we can imagine functionally preemptive causal systems in the case of rational agents. We can, therefore, imagine functionally preemptive causal systems in the case both of humans and of Cyborgs; and we can, similarly, imagine that not only Cyborgs but also humans are discovered to be machines. Thus, there are four cases to consider when attributing consciousness or mind:

1. A mechanical human
2. A functionally preemptive human
3. A mechanical Cyborg
4. A functionally preemptive Cyborg

Surely the nature of the causal system in this sense *is* properly connected to the attribution of consciousness or mind, or would be if one discovered that there are functionally preemptive systems. If it tuurned out, for example, that humans' brains embody functionally preemptive systems, whereas the Cyborg computer is a machine, we would have strong grounds indeed for suggesting that the human has mind whereas the Cyborg is a mere simulation of mind. We would have a reason to peek.

In order to see more clearly what's involved in the postulation of rational agents embodied in functionally preemptive causal systems, let's now look at the relation between the so-called agent causality theory of agency and the concept of a functionally preemptive system. I should add at this point that the clock paradigm for functional preemption is meant to be suggestive only. If functional preemption occurs in the brain, it will undoubtedly do so in some subtle form — as statistical patterns for physical events that can be accounted for only as responses to preceding functional states, for example.

Agent causality, as introduced by Richard Taylor (1966), is the causality exercised by an agent rather than by an event. The theory of agent causality is the theory that some objects — namely, agents — can be causes in their own right. Why did the arm move up? Because the agent caused it to move up. This answer is meant to replace the agency-neutered answer which says that events A, B, and C took place as a result of which D, the motion of the muscle in the arm, took place. Now the crucial question is whether agency causality is supposed to be inconsistent with event causality. If it is consistent with event causality, then statements that employ agency causality in accounting for events or actions are redescriptions of mechanical explanations; or, at the very least, the making of agency causality explanations does not preclude the possibility that the human is a machine. So long as agency causality accounts allow for mechanical explanations as well, agency causality will not provide a source of theory to those who would find a principle of the sort Searle needed but couldn't offer. Similarly, to the extent that we can determine, in the absence of a great deal of further work in cognitive science and neurophysiology, whether human beings operate by agency causality — that is, to the extent that the assessment of the agency causality theory is pretty much an *a priori* matter, as is the case with Chisholm's view of agent causality, for instance (1966) — agency causality will not help to justify the necessity of peeking in the attribution of consciousness or mind. If we know we have agency causality without having to determine whether our brain embodies any functionally preemptive elements, then we'll know that a Cyborg has it too. Agency causality theorists, then, must be prepared to give a fairly clear answer to the question of whether their theory pertains to functionally preemptive goings on. If it is an account of functionally preemptive goings on, then, the theory provides the philosophical groundwork for possible empirical discovery. Gustafson (1986, p. 162) to the contrary, the functionally preemptive version of agency causality is not at all inhospitable to the scientific attitude (see also Lycan 1987, p. 2). It positively requires scientific confirmation; and until there is such, it is as speculative and unfounded a view of human agency as would be the view that clocks ring at the time set because the function of setting them preempts the physics associated with the alarm mechanisms. We might be surprised to discover the occurrence of preemptive systems but the theory is a scientific one. A radical agency causality thesis that attempts to straddle the question of functional preemption will be split asunder by the fence it sits on.

John Thorp's (1980) recent account, for instance, seems to fail on this point. Thorp concludes that it is coherent to suppose there are two fundamentally distinct forms of causation: radical agency causation and event causation. But he doesn't seem to notice that if radical agency causation is to be basic, then certain physical regularities will be violated whenever agency causality occurs. It is not simply that there will be those goings on that work by event causality, and those goings on that work by agency causality; rather, since the agent is embodied in matter, a violation somewhere along the event causation chain must occur if the agency causation is to have purchase on the physical system. It follows that the libertarian's radical agency postulate is the postulate of a functionally preemptive causal system, and this is a scientific postulate. Thorp seems unfortunately oblivious of this: "The libertarian will pay anything, of course, to avoid compatibilism; the cost, roughly is that we need two primitives where we had one before" (p. 119). The cost, alas, is much greater than that, for the scientist will be very curious indeed as to the precise point at which the functional preemption takes place in the brain. Functional preemption will of course be localized and specific if it occurs, and, like every empirical thesis, is subject to confirmation. To defend libertarianism requires a great deal more than supplying a defense of the coherence of an empirical postulate presented as though it were a philosophical account.

The second point to observe concerning the relation between functional preemption and the notion of agent causality is this: Although any notion of radical or basic agent causality requires that the agent be embodied in a system with some functional preemption of physics, not any system with functional preemption of physics will be a system embodying rational agency. The paradigm with which we introduced the notion of a functionally preemptive system — the clock that rings according to its external alarm set rather than its internal alarm set — is not a rational agent, however magical or miraculous its functional preemption of physics makes it appear to be.

From this it might be argued that since a clock's embodiment in a functionally preemptive system would not suffice to make it a conscious agent, neither should the fact of embodiment of an apparent rational agent in a functionally preemptive system make a difference in our attribution of consciousness. This, however, does not follow: For although rational agency may be attributed on the basis of externally testable behavior alone, the wonders of discovering functional preemption in nature would surely be thought to connect in an important way somehow with the wonders of being conscious, as opposed to being a content-less or utterly preconscious (zombie-like or trance-like) rational agent.

Moreover, although a clock's embodiment in a functionally preemptive system would not make it a conscious agent, some might hold that this fact alone points to a strong connection between some mind somewhere and the clock. In any case, the practical point surely would be in the anticipation that if there should happen to be anything at all like functional preemption, it would not be in non-agent systems such as clocks, however clearly and distinctly we may conceive of such set-ups. If there is functional preemption and it does occur only in rational agents, then, following the line of analysis developed in Part 1, one might expect there also to be rational agents embodied in mechanical systems. And in that situation one would surely want to make the contrast count in the attribution of mind.

The long and short of it is that a principle that justifies peeking in the attribution of consciousness after PAL and behavioral checks have been made is *a priori* available.

But is there any evidence that the human brain has any functionally preemptive aspects? As astounding as it may seem, there is one neurophysiologist who has suggested there is — namely, Sir John Eccles. For example, in discussing the performance of nerve cells of the supplementary motor area (SMA) in the voluntary activity of monkeys, he goes so far as to state that , "we have here an irrefutable demonstration that a mental act of intention *initiates* the burst of discharges of a nerve cell" (Eccles and Robinson 1985, p. 162). This 'irrefutable demonstration' depends on there being no physical stimuli effecting the SMA discharges. "It is important to recognize that this burst of discharges of the observed SMA cell was not triggered by some other nerve cell of the SMA or elsewhere in the brain" (p. 162). The conclusion that Eccles believes is warranted from the data is that mind-brain interactionist dualism is true; these data constitute evidence for that theory.

On the face of it, Eccles appears to have made two conceptual errors here. The first is a confusion of evidence for functional preemption in a system with evidence for mind-brain interactionist dualism. The data he reviews relate to the occurrence of functionally apt but physically spontaneous goings on; if the interpretation of the data is correct, we could have evidence for functional preemption. But the leap from functional preemption to mind-brain interactionist dualism requires a bridging argument. To see this we need only consider the case of the functionally preemptive clock that always rings in accordance with the external alarm set. We can imagine having evidence that some clock was functionally preemptive in this way, but such evidence would not lead us to conclude that the clock was a conscious agent much less that it was a conscious agent whose mind was a distinct entity from its body. Or to put this another way, evidence for functional preemption in a system can be as much acknowledged by identity theorists as by dualists. Indeed, evidence for functional preemption might be quite welcome by some identity theorists because it could provide the basis for a distinction between those physical entities that are minds and those physical entities that are not minds.

However, our interest here is in the evidence for the occurrence of functional preemption. So the first error is not germane; interpretation of the data is. The problem on this score is that Eccles has slid from absence of evidence of cause to evidence of absence of cause. At the moment we have no adequate physical account of the triggering of discharge of the observed SMA cell. But there are still three possibilities: (1) There is an adequate physical trigger of the discharge that we have not yet located; (2) there is a violation of independently established neurochemical regularities; and (3) there is an indeterminacy spillover from the quantum level to the cell level such that these discharges are accountable by statistical means only. Neither (1) nor (3) would indicate any functional preemption; and to discriminate between (2) and the other two possibilities requires specific evidence of the point of purchase of the preemption. And Eccles, of course, has provided nothing of the kind. Moreover, in other accounts of the same data, he is considerably more guarded in tone: "The subtlety and complexity of the patterns written in space and time by this 'enchanted loom' of Sherrington's and the emergent properties of this system are beyond any levels of investigation by physics or physiology at the present time . . . and perhaps for a long time to come. I would postulate that in the liaison areas these neuronal patterns of module activity are the receiving stations or antennae for the ongoing operations in the consciousness of World 2 (the conscious self)" (Eccles 1976, p. 117). Here his conclusions are presented as a highly tentative postulate, hardly the result of 'irrefutable demonstration'. So we have an area cut out for further investigation with regard to the possibility of functional preemption; but we do not, as yet, have evidence of functional preemption.

A similar story concerns Eccles's conclusions from Libet's work on the subjective timing of conscious experience in relation to neuronal events (Libet 1978; Libet et al, 1979). Eccles writes, "direct stimulation of the somaesthetic cortex results in a conscious experience after a delay as long as 0.5s for weak stimulation, and a similar delay is observed for a sharp, but weak, peripheral skin stimulus . . . [A]lthough there is this delay in experiencing the peripheral stimulus, it is actually judged to be much earlier, at about the time of cortical arrival of the afferent input . . . This antedating procedure does not seem to be explicable by any neurophysiological process. Presumably it is a strategy that has been learnt by the self-conscious mind" (Eccles and Popper 1977, p. 364). Once again Eccles has been quick to interpret data as evidence for dualist interactionism.

Patricia S. Churchland (1981) has pointed out several ways in which the Libet results might be interpreted otherwise; indeed, she has taken pains to discover how the data themselves might be unreliable. Libet (1981) disputes her objections, but in the course of doing so firmly yanks the carpet from under Eccles's feet: "Subjective referral in time violates no neurophysiological principles or data and is compatible with the theory of 'mental' and 'physical' correspondence" (p. 182). Our earlier observation bears repeating here too: Our difficulties explicating neurophysiological events and the various data concerning and surrounding them must, first and foremost, be taken to be indicative of our general ignorance about the brain, and *not* as evidence of the absence of explications of these data with reference to neurophysiological processes.

All in all we must conclude that we have no genuine evidence for functional preemption in the brain. However, the conception of functional preemption illustrates the availability of a principle that would justify peeking in the attribution of consciousness and intentional content. Arguments such as those of Patricia Churchland (1986) concerning what we've called a Cyborg — arguments which conclude that "if its behavioral output is a product of its complex internal system of representations implemented in its brain, then its utterances have meaning in exactly the way mine do" (p. 345) — are incomplete, depending as they do on there being no causal set- ups that are neither mechanistic nor probabilistic. I assume that Churchland would cheerfully accept this qualification, since the point presents yet another angle on the potential limitations of the view that computational psychological models are fully autonomous from the neuroscience that investigates the means of realization of the functional algorithms (Pylyshyn 1984; Churchland 1986, Chapter 9). The main upshot of thought experiments concerning functionally preemptive clocks, then, is to reinforce the naturalist rather than the strictly top-down or rationalist methodology.

One further caution: The clock paradigm points to a form of gross functional preemption. But even if some clear correlation were found to exist between certain functional states of the brain and the probability that certain cells will discharge, where the only physicalist accounts for the discharging of the cells is randomly probabilistic independent of any correlation with functional states or engrams, that would still be enough to call into question the attribution of consciousness to a Cyborg that was strictly mechanistic, or mechanistic-probabilistic with no such quasi-functionally preemptive element.

There also exist other forms of relationship between the functional and the physical that, while not involving preemption, might disturb the neatly mechanistic, or mechanistic plus probabilistic account of the brain. For example, the brain's system of encoding may be sufficiently rich that to describe the code is more or less as open-ended as to describe the environment that has been encoded. An account of the brain that features a distinction between 'bounded' and 'unbounded' encodings or engrams might well have this feature (Harnad 1982). So might accounts featuring the hologram-like system of brain encoding or the image-making aspects of representation (Pribram et al 1974; Johnson-Laird 1983). Although we might find no preemptive elements, and although we might discover that all the goings on at the neurochemical level preserve mechanistic predictability during brain functioning, it might in principle be impossible to present an account of how those goings on accomplish the representational functions of the brain, since the latter are as open-ended as our descriptions of the world itself.

Furthermore, the continual re-representation by the brain of its engrams using non-natural or acquired concepts, or constructed concepts, can only compound the open-endedness. It's a bit like trying to discover how a mirror accomplishes its mirroring and all we can see is the world depicted in the mirror. We might call such a system a *functionally opaque representational mirror;* we couldn't say how it functions, though we might hold it to be a mechanism. Still, humans might be functionally opaque whereas the Cyborg is functionally accountable (transparent), thus possibly justifying attribution of mind to the human and not to the Cyborg.

So, can we attribute consciousness to a Cyborg without peeking at the way its material structure embodies its functional organization? The answer we have come to is that we don't quite know yet. The view that we can, like the view that we can't, has empirical content, or assumes an empirical hypothesis. If the brain is a machine, then we'd have no available grounds on which to assert that Cyborgs are not conscious whereas humans are. If the brain is neither a machine nor a mechanistic-probabilistic entity, then we might have the grounds on which to withhold the attribution of consciousness to a mechanical Cyborg and hold that it "sees" but does not see, has ears with which it "hears" but does not hear, "experiences" but does not experience, and so on. However the main point that needs stressing is that the strength of the grounds that would justify withholding attribution of consciousness to a Cyborg seems to be inversely proportional to the likelihood of our ever coming to have such grounds.

Consciousness Attribution to any PAL Short of the Cyborg

Debates among theorists have sometimes centered so much on the implications of functional isomorphy that the implications of what might be called *functional simimorphy*, the functional resemblances of two systems to each other, have been ignored. To the extent that integrated system programming of the sort contemplated in Part 1 is realizable and elaborable, the abstract problems of functional simimorphy will be instantiated in actual models. And chief among these problems is the apparent unavailability of any principle whereby we may determine whether some language-learning, language-using, independent-purpose-holding rational homunculus that, in other respects, is unlike a human is merely pre-consciously aware and contentless, so to speak, or, on the other hand, truly conscious, conscious in the strong sense.

When we have functional isomorphy as a given, the problem of consciousness attribution is suitably narrow and, as I have tried to argue, amenable to a reasonably clear and elegant solution. But when we don't have functional isomorphy, and do have something that meets our rational agency tests, we discover how many-sided or many-factored consciousness attribution can be. For example, if it is true that conscious awareness in the human is associated with learning new tasks and preconscious awareness is associated with the performance of routinized tasks, does this mean that any rational agent (artificial, extraterrestrial, or whatever) will tend to be truly conscious when it learns? How could we tell if its learning is accomplished automatically? How might we discern whether its learning is a performance with the same degree of conscious attentiveness one has to information absorbed subliminally — namely, none? Is a device or organism that has no need for offline processing — and hence (if Winson [1985] is right) no need for the kind of sleeping information processing that humans have, and hence no sleeping and waking cycles at all — always as though awake, or always as though asleep? Our theories seem to us to be powerful instruments when they give us answers to questions such as would system A, which is functionally isomorphic to system B, but realized differently, be awake when system B is awake? But they are woefully inadequate when dealing with the question of the relation between wakefulness and consciousness say, and we're only challenged to do that through the theory of functional simimorphy or the general theory of rational agency.

Similarly, problems of consciousness attribution to PALs whose functioning falls short of the Cyborg point to the tensions in our notions of consciousness itself — tensions we need not face when considering consciousness attribution to the ideal Cyborg. There are two main areas of strain at the moment, and in both cases additional pressure against the concept is resulting from empirical work. First is the notion of the unity of consciousness — a foggy business to begin with, but even more puzzling since the 1960s and 1970s, when commissurotomy, or split-brain, patients were being studied (Nagel 1975; Churchland 1986, Chapter 5). And second is the apparent radical ambiguity in the notion of consciousness, given that it is intended to mean both attentiveness and only a specific sort of attentiveness. The distinction here is between conscious awareness and preconscious awareness, as it might crudely be put, or between what one is attending to *and* what one experiences oneself as attending to on the one hand, and what one is attending to but not experiencing oneself as attending to on the other hand (negotiating curves while driving, say, but concentrating on a conversation with the passenger or absorbed in the music on the radio) (Dennett 1969, Chapter 6).

Additional wedges are being driven into this distinction by discoveries concerning the range, depth, and methods of preconscious processing. It's one thing to be able to put one's attention to matters other than what one is seeing; one's attention can come back and one will experience oneself as seeing those things. It's another thing altogether to realize that some damage to the visual cortex produces blindsight. In general, much more information is processed through the senses, on through the cerebral processing system, and used by the response processes directly without going through conscious awareness than had previously been recognized (Dixon 1981; Johnson-Laird 1983, pp. 465-470). This empirical observation aggravates the already troublesome concern that any simulation short of the ideal Cyborg might be conscious in the weak sense (i.e., preconscious only) and never conscious in the strong sense. And no one at the moment has any theoretical machinery appropriate to this problem.

On these matters, theorists with naturalist, rationalist, intentional-attributivist, and causal-power materialist leanings will each find a spot within the theory that allows for postponement of such questions, pending the ongoing work in cognitive science. And that work includes, of course, the bootstrapping efforts of philosophers struggling to reach for solutions to these problems a step ahead and a step behind this or that piece of empirical or formal work in cognitive science.

8

Degrees of Consciousness

We will now briefly consider the attribution of consciousness to artificial rational agents whose functioning falls short of the ideal Cyborg, under the assumption that neuroscience does *not* yield conceptually challenging causal set-ups in the brain such as functional or quasi-functional preemption.

It would be convenient if we had a generally acceptable theory of degrees of consciousness in nonhuman animals, for that is one area in which similar problems have been encountered in practice. However, it is not only the case that no such theory exists, but the scientific study of conscious thought in nonhuman animals has been meager with a few exceptions such as Griffin (1984).

And even if work along these lines were available, there is the awkward application difficulty: We tend to attribute ever more consciousness to animals as they function more and more rationally. But the design of our PAL shows us that rational agency is independent of various features that have been present throughout biological evolution from a certain point on and which are strongly associated with the presence of consciousness. We associate consciousness with wakefulness, for example. And since the higher animals have waking and sleeping cycles, we look primarily for signs of waking rationality in our attribution of consciousness to them. But with artificial agents and robots we have the reverse problem. As we've seen, we can build robots that (who) are very advanced in their rationality but primitive or altogether lacking in wake/sleep rhythms; and in such cases we are at a loss as to whether we should judge these robots to be always sleeping or always awake. Similarly, mammals show plenty of signs of an affective life. They exhibit fondness, hostility, fear, boldness, playfulness, and even shame. They are cute when young just as human babies are. And as we personally remember something of the nature of consciousness from an early age — often from a pre-linguistic stage of life — it is easy for us to attribute something of the same sort of consciousness to such animals as well, especially when rational interagency attributions are made by them. But our problem with robots is the reverse. We can build a robot with a high degree of rational interagency attribution, language learning, and so on, but with no or hardly any affective life. We are stymied when we try to disentangle affective life from rationality insofar as attribution of consciousness is concerned.

Application of the notion of conscious attention to robots encounters the same difficulty. We know from our own cases as humans that the learning of new behaviors requires conscious attention; once a behavior has become routinized, it can be performed without conscious attention. Yet conscious attention may also be directed toward even the most automatic of behaviors such as walking. We tend to think that animals will be most conscious when they are most challenged to learn or cope with a new situation, and our biological connection with the nonhuman animals supports this observation. But we have no biological connection with a rational interagency attributive robot, or will not have any when we build one; so instead of looking primarily for signs of rationality in the robot (which, as we've seen, we'll be able to find) we must discover some way of dealing with the question whether all *its* learning is automatic and, hence, not necessarily conscious.

We can also imagine building an android whose memory access works so differently from our own that difficult puzzles about its consciousness would emerge from consideration of its mental life. If a rational agent compubot were built that had, as we put it earlier, virtually no long-term memory of particular events, but which nevertheless had a powerful situation analyzer, it might be able to learn a great deal about its environment by comparing a particular event to the general rules it had already extracted without retaining any memory of the particular events from which it has extracted those generalizations. Consequently such a compubot would be able to deal effectively with its surroundings and communicate with language about its current situation, but it would have little sense of itself as having a continuous life. If the short-term memory access is sufficiently small, the mental life is reduced to zero, or would seem to be; yet its cognition or rational agency might be very elaborate. (For a discussion of human neuropathology yielding related problems, see Sachs 1985.)

Finally, at the very center of these issues is the question of the relation between rational agency and what we might call 'ego consciousness'. Perhaps the easiest way to introduce this notion is to consider the nature of those intuitions captured by statements such as "I'm *me*" or "How interesting: Every morning I wake up, and every morning I'm Leonard again!" It's one thing to hold an entirely objective picture of the world. Within such a picture there is a multitude of entities, and one of them is this person, one of them is that person over there and so on. It is another thing to recognize that one of them is "Me!" That is, into a totally objective picture of the world, a picture of a world with a multitude of entities all of which are metaphysically so to speak equal, we can introduce another, nonobjective, or 'unequal' feature. One of those entities is me!

By 'ego consciousness' or 'ego awareness' or 'the ego conscious stance', I mean the holding by a rational agent of a picture of the world of objects all of which are equal — except that one of them, and only one of them, is me. I take it that all humans have a sense of ego consciousness and, upon some reflection, will be familiar with the ability to switch perspectives from an entirely objective picture to one that includes the subjective ("But it's me!") in the overall image. The fact that we have the ability to employ both the objective and the ego conscious perspective, and to switch from one to the other may be brought out by consideration of how important decisions are made, for example. Say Gloria is trying to decide whether to marry Harold or Roger. On the one hand she may think objectively about this choice and, so to speak, give advice to herself on the basis of her observations concerning Harold, Roger, and herself, just as she would if she were giving advice to another person. On the other hand, it may suddenly occur to her, "Yes, but I'm me! This is my one and only life and its mine, and I must consider the question as *mine* as well."

We have all experienced moments of special and wondrous significance — moments when we are flooded with the realization that "I'm me!" James Joyce gives Stephen Daedelus a discovery of this kind in *Portrait of the Artist as a Young Man*. In this situation, it is an epiphany to realize, "I am Stephen Daedelus, living in County Cork, in Ireland . . . " and so on. And there are, to be sure, many people for whom the wondrous aspect of ego consciousness can be recalled or invoked virtually at will. There is a sense of the interesting, the peculiar, and the amazing associated with the ego conscious stance. "How *interesting*, how *peculiar*, how *amazing*, that of all the objects of the world I should find myself as one of them, this very person!" (See also Nagel 1979b; 1986.)

Now there is a strong relationship between our concept of self-consciousness and our concept of the ego conscious stance. Yet there is no reason to think that a mechanical rational agent of our construction will have the ability, or will even *appear* to have the ability, to adopt an ego conscious perspective over and above its objective picture of things unless we give it the ability (or apparent ability) to develop and use such a perspective.

On the one hand, any rational agent must have a concept of the person that it is. It must have a concept of the first person or, as we put it in Part 1, a concept of 'Agent-1'. And it must have the ability to apply this concept appropriately — that is, to itself. So in one sense it has a self-concept. But this self-concept is an entirely objective self-concept. Thus, and this is a fundamental point about the problem of consciousness attribution, there are two distinct notions of self-consciousness. On the one hand, there is the entirely objective notion of a rational agent with, necessarily, the ability to apply the first person concept to itself. On the other hand, there is the intuition of ego consciousness captured by such statements as "And this person is me!" On the one hand, then, there is the self-consciousness that any rational agent must have simply by virtue of its representational and information processing apparatus. It is about this 'self-consciousness' that we may still ask, "But is it *really* conscious?" And on the other hand, there is the self-consciousness of the ego conscious person. If we attribute ego consciousness to some being, we no longer need to ask, "But is this being *really* conscious?" (To attribute ego conscious *behavior* to some agent is or is not the attribution of ego consciousness to it depending on one's view of the relation of behavior to consciousness. Here we're merely calling attention to the difference between something's being a rational agent and something's being, in addition, ego conscious.)

An interesting question is whether we will ever be able to include an 'ego consciousness developmental program' in an artificial rational agent. On this question, we seem to have no reason to consider it impossible to devise such a program. Indeed, we might already be able to envision in very broad terms what such a program would involve. To begin with, a rational agent would have an innate first person or Agent-1 concept. In addition, a rational agent might be given a free-floating self-identification unit: At the onset, everything is identified as self or might be identified as self so long as it is present to consciousness or present to current attention. As well, there will be a subunit of the self-identification program that looks for continuities. Gradually, self would come to be identified with that object that is continuously present to current attention. Since it is the first person, or Agent-1, that is the object continuously present to current attention, Agent-1 would come to be identified as self.

Another subunit of the self-identification program associates a special form of pleasure with the successful completion of self-identification searches. That is, part of the motivation of the rational agent is to complete the identification of self with an object. Accordingly, the reflection, or calling to attention of the self-identification with the first person or Agent-1, is attended by pleasure. Furthermore, if a rational agent searches its memory very deeply and recalls to consciousness its earliest free-floating self-identification, this will complete a different self identification task, which itself will be attended by special pleasure. Thus a robot might be given a program enabling it to exclaim, "This robot is just this robot, but I am the cosmos!" and to be pleased with its mysticism.

I digress. Here we are primarily concerned with the problem of consciousness attribution to a rational agent that (who) does not develop ego consciousness but, instead, is capable only of operating from a purely objective self-identification. Surely, we are tempted to say, having a first-person concept in the way any rational agent must have does not guarantee or suffice for the having of true consciousness.

What, then, do we make of these problems? An easy solution is to say that affective life, attention span, wakefulness, development of ego consciousness, and, of course, sophistication of rationality all constitute consciousness factors; and the more of these a rational agent has, the more secure our consciousness attribution to it can be. This rather simple approach should not be spurned merely because it is obvious. These factors are co-present in our own consciousness, and we take it that our self-consciousness consists in their co-presence in us. Accordingly, self-consciousness can be seen *not* to be an all-or-nothing phenomenon, a light that is either shining or not: rather, it is a phenomenon that is present in factors. Moreover, the co-presence in us of a variety of consciousness related factors should not lead us to conclude that these factors are not relatively independent, nor that consciousness itself does not accrue by degrees with their inclusion in a rational agent.

Yet there are some questions that become more rather than less troublesome by such a solution. Say, for example, that we build an emotionless robot that is purely objectively functioning but conceptually very sophisticated in its language learning, and its ability to assess its situation. And suppose someone wants to erase all its memories. Suppose further that the robot holds its own survival as a goal and that its innate survival goal has been replaced by its learned concept of 'survival'. Would it now be morally indifferent to go against the express wishes of the robot and erase all of its memories? Does the robot have rights on its own, and not just by virtue of its being of value *to* humans? To hold that consciousness accrues by degrees does not help here, for what's required, it seems, is arbitration between the view that moral status is to be accorded to any language-learning, language-using rational agent on the one hand, and the view that moral status requires the ability to engage in the particular forms of psychological empathy and identification that can only be found in ego conscious persons, on the other.

If we're content to let these issues remain contentious, we should nonetheless recognize that practical social issues will require practical resolutions despite theoretical controversy. If a robot with a high degree of sophistication in rationality but a very low degree of affective life and ego consciousness requests moral consideration, should that consideration be given? At this stage of the game, such questions are daunting indeed.

But we should also remember that moral intuitions and legal precedents are forged from a stew of practical experience. In addition, new areas of science and technology tend to create their own special set of moral intuitions and legal principles. Cruelty to (nonhuman) animals is a different sort of charge from causing harm to humans. Would it be fudging, then, to suggest that "erasing the memories of a compubot in an unauthorized manner" might be a charge arising from a special set of attitudes that people develop toward artificial, inorganic, rational agents? Even the creator of a compubot might be charged under such a law; similarly, we can conceive of an artist being prevented by society from destroying one of his own works of art on the grounds that the piece's value to posterity outweighs the natural rights of the artist over his or her own creation. (For related discussions, see Lieber 1985; and Turkle 1984.)

9

Conclusion

We now have a procedural solution to our question, "Can a machine be conscious?" To attribute consciousness to some entity, we follow the following procedure. We ask:

1. Is this entity a rational agent? That is, does this entity have (a) independent purpose regardless of its contact with other agents, (b) the ability to make what we've called interagency attributions on a pure or natural basis? And does it in addition have (c) the ability to learn from scratch significant portions of some natural language, and the ability to use these elements in satisfying its purposes and those of its interlocutors? If the entity does not meet these criteria, then the attribution of consciousness to it will be at best dubious. The only plausible circumstances in which some consciousness might nevertheless be attributed to beings that do not fully meet these criteria are those involving biologically related species or organisms or devices constructed similarly to organisms or devices that meet not only these three elements but the other considerations to follow as well. Thus being able to meet the criteria of point 1 is a necessary condition for consciousness attribution.

2. Are there any paradigmatically conscious beings such as humans who have functionally preemptive causal systems? If so, does a device that meets the criteria of point 1 also have functionally preemptive elements in the material embodiment of its cognitive processor? If the device does not have these elements whereas the paradigmatically conscious beings do, then there are grounds on which to withhold consciousness attributions to it. On the other hand, if the paradigmatically conscious beings do not have functionally preemptive causal systems, then the lack of same in the entities in question, or the differences in their material base,

or the differences in the manner in which they carry out cognitive functions from humans, cannot be held to be grounds for withholding consciousness attributions from them. As to the question of how to treat this issue in the absence of adequate understanding of the human brain, it would seem that only positive evidence of as unusual and miraculous an arrangement such as functional preemption would be grounds to work from. Assumptions such as Searle's, that the material base of brain consciousness will be discovered to be as far removed from mechanism as quantum physics is from Newtonian mechanics, is not at the moment justified, to put it mildly.

3. On the assumption that the human brain is a system in which physics creates or serves function, then some consciousness may be attributed to any system that fully meets the three criteria of point 1. As I've argued in Part 1, we're already in a position to build machines that meet those criteria; hence we're also in a position to build machines with some degree of consciousness (so long as the above assumption holds true). However, we must also ask, "Does the entity exhibit various consciousness-associated factors such as emotional life, wakefulness, a sense of continuity with its past, and the development of the ego conscious stance?" The more it does so, the more degrees of consciousness may be attributed to it.

As for the moral rights of machines to which consciousness has been attributed on these grounds, only practical experience with such machines — together with continuing philosophical analysis — will yield determinations of these matters. But there is little doubt that the granting of moral rights to artificial intelligences, including language-learning and language-using independently purposive PALs, will be extremely parsimonious for a long time to come.

PART THREE

The Mystic's Project

10

A Dialogue

If it turns out that the human brain operates according to straightfor-wardly mechanical principles, then we will have no doubt at all that a machine can be conscious. Humans would then have been discovered to be machines, and humans are undoubtedly conscious. *Ergo*, some machines are conscious. But it is by no means clear to us *how* machines have consciousness. Nor is it clear how the human body can have the attribute of being conscious.

The question may have two emphases in particular:

1. How can a *machine* be conscious? How can something whose every state is in principle predictable, given its earlier states and those of its environment, have the sort of consciousness a human has, since the human's consciousness includes an awareness or a sense of radical freedom of choice?
2. How can *any material thing* be conscious? How can some merely mechanical material arrangement of particles have this wondrous phenomenon of self-awarenesss?

In the following dialogue between a Mystic and a Philosopher, I present the Mystic's account of how matter can have consciousness and how a machine can freely choose. Nothing in what follows is in any way implied directly by, or required for, the views that have already been presented. Rather, this material is included as a sort of dessert. Like many desserts it may be too cloying for the tastes of some. If so, apologies from the chef. In any case, the dessert portion has been kept suitably bite-sized so that a sample may be had and 'seconds' discreetly refused.

PHILOSOPHER: How can a machine, which is a mere concatenation of bits of matter, be conscious?

MYSTIC: Easy. All matter is conscious. A stone is conscious. So of course a machine can be conscious.

P: A stone is conscious? That sounds preposterous. Do you think the stone is thinking about something? What sorts of thoughts does a stone have?

M: A stone does not have thoughts. The difficulty you're having is that you assume that if something is conscious, then that thing is a personal entity or a rational agent. What you're missing is the notion of 'impersonal consciousness'.

P: Alright, swami, explain.

M: Happily. You take it that your mind is your body's because when your mind plans to move your foot, the movement of your foot follows, whereas if your mind plans to have the sun jump in the sky, the jumping of the sun does not follow. You identify your mind with a certain body because of the routine connection of certain mental events with certain bodily motions. This identification is based on diachronic experience. It is through repeated sequences of the appropriate kind that you identify your personal consciousness with your personal body. So far so good?

P: Yes.

M: Now there is another mode of identification that does not involve diachronic criteria of application. The base synchronic (or at-the-moment) identification of the object that has consciousness is not personal at all. Indeed, it cannot be personal at root since the concept of a person has no scope at the moment. For something to be a person, it must exhibit a certain form of sequence relating mental to physical events (bodily motions corresponding to plans). Based on such sequences, we come to form an image of a particular body as a person, or as the body of a certain person. Once we've done this, we can say that, at moment t_n, the person is at P. In this sense we can locate a person at a moment.

But this is synchronic personal identity which is derivative of the diachronic identification. However, there is a level of synchronic identity of the object that has 'this consciousness', which is logically prior to the application of any diachronic personal criterion. To discover this sense, consider that there is nothing about any bit of matter — an arm, or a leg, an eye, or an ear, a torso, or scalp and hair — which shows that it is or is not currently part of a body that has mind. There is nothing about the arm on your body which marks it as matter that is part of a material system that has mind, compared with the arm sitting in a vat of formaldehyde marking it as matter that is not part of a physical system with mind.

Moment by moment, then, any bit of matter might have mind. The stone might have mind.

P: The stone *might* have mind, but whether it does or not depends on whether it's part of a physical system that exhibits rational agency.

M: Yes; whether it has *personal* mind depends on that. But now consider that at any moment it is appropriate to ask, "Is there mind here?" and to answer, "Yes! There is mind here." And if we ask, 'Which mind?' we needn't refer to a mind identified as a rational agent. We can say 'This mind!' or 'My mind', irrespective of the plans being followed by the appropriate motions.

P: Do you mean, if paralysis were to suddenly develop, there would or might still be experience and thoughts, and therefore 'this mind'?

M: I didn't quite mean that, but we can pick the question up from the case. Say one were to be suddenly paralyzed. What matter would be appropriate to identify as my body? Is this not an arbitrary or free judgment? One might then identify the whole cosmos as one's body; or one might identify the body that used to work in personal sequences; or one might identify no matter at all as the matter to which my mind belongs. And at the deepest synchronic level, it is a matter of indifference as to whether one is paralyzed, or has total plan-to-motion potency over the whole cosmos, or has merely partial plan-to-bodily-motion potency over a certain stretch of the cosmos — namely, the personal body. There is always this mind, or my mind, and it might be identified or not identified with anything, including a stone.

P: I'm going to have to think about that a bit. I'm not sure about this 'deepest synchronic level' talk.

M: Consider the opposite case to that of paralysis: total potency of plan-to-motion. One *might* suddenly discover that one had the ability to plan for the sun to flip somersaults, and the sun flips somersaults. One *might* suddenly discover that the whole cosmos was one's personal body. This is logically possible. If it were to occur, one would identify the cosmos as the physical system with which this mind or my mind is identified.

P: But it's not that way.

M: It hasn't been that way in the past, no. But it might suddenly become that way at any moment. This calls attention to the fact that there is nothing specific about the stones and rivers and trees that makes them in some sense unsuitable to be objects that have mind. Moreover, and much more to the point, when one attends to the root synchronic perspective, one holds in suspension one's past information concerning the plan-to-motion sequences that were successful and those that were not. One attends to the equality of all matter with respect to this mind. And with attention to the equality of all matter with respect to this mind, one comes to recognize with startling clarity the freedom to identify the whole cosmos as the body of this mind or my mind.

P: This discussion is doing me no good, I'm afraid. I don't recognize anything of this kind, not even with murky obscurity.

M: ....

P: Hello?

M: ....Mm?

P: What were you doing?

M: Identifying with the cosmos. (He picks up a bottle of correction fluid.) See this?

P: Yes.

M: This is part of me, you know.

P: Really!

M: Yes. So is this, and this, and this (he points to the typewriter, the wall, the carpet.) Of course, these are not parts of the person who is speaking to you, but they are parts of me.

P: I wasn't aware that there could be a difference between the referent of the first person pronoun and the first person.

M: (laughs) Whatever grammarian called 'I' the first-person pronoun created a lot of confusion for philosophers. 'I' should have been called the self-referring pronoun.

P: What's the difference?

M: The difference is that we are comfortable with the use of self-concepts in reference to impersonal objects. For example, we talk about a chair sitting by *itself* on the floor, or a gun firing by *itself*. Every thing has self-identity, or is identical with itself; but that doesn't imply that every object is a person. Thus 'I', a self-referring term, can refer to an impersonal or suprapersonal object (i.e., one that includes persons as proper subparts) such as the cosmos. But when 'I' functions as a first-person pronoun, it must refer to a person.

P: Have we gotten lost in a thicket of words?

M: Probably. The point is that the speaker can use 'I' to refer to this mind-body; and this mind-body need not constitute a personal unit. The speaker can maintain a concept of the first person that is the speaker simultaneous with a concept of self, or this mind, the body of which is identified as the whole cosmos.

P: Ah, so the whole cosmos is I, but the speaker is just the little old speaker.

M: Right.

P: Hmm..........I have the outline of the concepts, but I'm afraid they don't hold any power for me. They don't speak to me with any experiential resonance.

M: That's hardly surprising.

P: Now you're going to suggest I take up cross-legged meditation?

M: Oh no. I wouldn't do that!

P: Whew. Well, then, where does that leave us?

M: I was trying to explain to you how any old stone not only might have mind but actually has mind. And I hope that now you can see both aspects of this. First, there's nothing specific about a bit of matter that makes it suitable for having personal mind. Second, all matter is synchronically equal with respect to this mind or my mind. Every bit of matter is part of the object that has this mind or my mind. A rather simple way to look at it, if you prefer, is to reflect that we can unit our physical systems any way we please. We can regard this body plus that body, or this bit of matter and that bit of matter, as a single physical system. Then, even though this body has the muscles that move when my mind plans for them to move, and the rest of the universe is not similarly responsive to my personal mind's plans, I can nevertheless regard the whole universe as a single physical system and identify it as the object that has this mind or my mind. There is no need to use the criterion for the identification of a person's body in the identification of the object that has the mind that is currently conscious of itself.

P: Echoes of Descartes, Husserl, Sartre, Spinoza?

M: And Sankara, Sakyamuni, Nagarjuna, Dogen and many others too, no doubt.

P: However, you started by saying a stone has no thoughts. Now it turns out a stone has your thoughts, or my thoughts.

M: Not quite. Does your arm have your thoughts? No. Your arm is part of the body to which your mind is attributed. And the stone is part of the body to which my mind, or this mind, may be attributed, and that body is the whole cosmos. However, it is only the speaker's body to which these thoughts are to be attributed. We can keep the personal and impersonal referents clear. The speaker has thoughts and a limited personal body, two arms, two legs, and so on. But I am the cosmos. I am not the speaker. I am not a single person. I include many persons, billions of them, in fact; and I include billions of impersonal objects — stones, trees, flowers, planets, stars. And I am mind. And the speaker is aware only of the speaker's thoughts. And I, the cosmos, am not aware in a personal way of any thoughts, even though my mind includes the thoughts not only of the speaker but also of every other person in the cosmos . . . You're shaking your head.

P: I think I've been reduced to Transcendental Speechlessness.

M: Ready for a change of subject?

P: Suits me fine. But just before we go on, could you connect this once again to the topic of how a machine can have mind?

M: The main point, once again, is that when we attribute mind to a body, we are always attributing the magic of consciousness to some old inert lump of matter. So what scientists do or do not discover about the workings of the matter to which mind is attributed is not important, really. There is always this absurd connection, if you like, whereby mind is attributed to or placed with some inert lump of matter. Finally, careful meditation — I hesitate to use the word — on this absurd attribution of mind to body leads one to discover the perspective whereby there is only one mind, this mind, the mind of the cosmos, and many rational agents or persons within the cosmos, for each of which (whom) there is, in another sense, a mind, a personal mind, attributed to a specific body. Moreover . . .

P: Excuse me, can I take you up on your offer to change the subject?

M: Sorry.

P: What about mechanism, freedom, and self-consciousness? Does the Mystic have any special insights into the free will/determinism problem?

M: Probably.

P: Can you do a little better than that?

M: I'm sure I can. I can do anything that is logically possible to do, and I guess it's logically possible to improve on that answer.

P: What do you mean you can do anything?

M: I mean just that. I can do anything that's logically possible. I can jump to the moon. I can transform myself into a spider and then back again into this human form. I can make the typewriter float and I can make the keys type without touching my fingers to them. Whatever. I can do anything.

P: Seriously?

M: Seriously.

P: Would you like to make a demonstration?

M: Sure. What would you like to see?

P: I'd like to see the typewriter float.

M: All right. Ready?

P: Ready.

M: Okay. Here goes. (He closes his eyes. The typewriter does not float.) Oh, well, it didn't happen that time.

P: Has it *ever* happened?

M: I've never tried to make a typewriter float before.

P: Is there anything *unusual*, anything *extraordinary* that you have been able to do?

M: Oh yes, I've done so many *amazing* things. Watch. I'm going to move my arm. (He moves his arm.) Isn't that amazing! I plan to move my arm, and my arm moves!

P: You're an easily amazed person.

M: Yes. That there is a world is amazing. That it has pattern is amazing. That I am here is amazing. That everything is as it is is amazing. Suchness: amazing! And the discovery that the human being is a machine would not affect the intuition of amazement at all. For what is amazing is the experience of spontaneity, that things are just as they are, that they happen the way they do. I was interested in your discussion of functional preemption, for instance. To me, there is nothing more or less amazing about a functionally preemptive system than a mechanical system. It is this imaginably-otherwise-but-actually-this-way at the heart of every pattern that is amazing. And precisely because both functional preemption and mechanism are conceivable as discoveries concerning the human, each would be accompanied by an equal sense of amazement on my part if it were actual.

P: We've drifted into amazement, but what I was asking was whether you've ever done something *unusual* — that is, contrary to the usual patterns, such as planning for the typewriter to float, then having it float. Surely there's a difference between amazement at the everyday pattern, everyday causality, on the one hand, and amazement at that which defies the usual patterns on the other hand.

M: There's a conceptual difference between the two sorts of events, but the amazement shouldn't be any different. However, you wanted me to get off amazement and onto the unusual. Have I done anything that defies the usual causal pattern? To be frank, no. But that does not prevent me from experiencing my omnipotence. I can do *anything*. I can jump to the moon, I can transform myself into a spider and then back into a human again, I can make the typewriter float . . .

P: We've been here before, haven't we?

M: Of course. We are always at precisely the same place. We are at the point at which any event might be followed by any other logically possible event. The thought might arise: "Let the typewriter float!" And the typewriter might just float. We are always at such a point of omnipotentiality, which is the only true content of our experience-right-now of potency.

   Simultaneously, then, I experience (1) omnipotentiality and (2) the thought arising, for example, "Let's see if the typewriter will float: Float typewriter." Simultaneously, the next moment, I experience (1) omnipotentiality, and (2) the perception of the typewriter not floating, with the thought, "Nope, didn't work," and so on. So I may as well say "I can't do anything at all" as that "I can do anything at all." Would you like to see my total incapacity?

P: How could you *show* me that?

M: Easy. You do something bad to me, to prove that I'll react in the normal way, and then you'll demonstrate that I can do something. (Thus, you'll prove me wrong.) On the other hand, if I helplessly let you do it, I'll have proven that I'm not capable of controlling anything. Now then, sweep your arm so that it moves toward my eye.

(P sweeps his arm so it moves towards M's eye.)

M: (Blinking) Oops. The blink happened. I didn't control it though.

P: And so whatever happens you'll say that it just happened, that you didn't control it.

M: Isn't it so? Even when thoughts occur, "better move my body, better avoid that punch" and so on, these thoughts *just occur*. And the appropriate bodily motions *just follow*. How well aware I am that all my agency is perfectly fused with what just spontaneously happens to me. My thoughts happen to me. My plans occur within me unbidden. And corresponding bodily motions just follow.

P: And your choices *just occur* too.

M: When we reflect that there is only actuality and the logically possible, then we recognize both that we can do anything and that we can do nothing. The word 'can' I suppose had best be struck from our vocabulary. We'd be much better off without it. There are those things that have happened, there are those patterns to which the events have added up, and there is the order of the logically possible. But we need not think of our predictions of the future as anything more than current activities of ours. When we stop justifying our predictions by appealing to what is empirically possible, or what we can do as opposed to what we can't do, then we experience the fusion of agency and spontaneity. . . . Are you with me?

P: Yes. . . . I was just struck for a moment with the fact that we suddenly seem to have arrived on topic.

M: That's right. Showing the compatibility of mechanism and respon-sibility or choice is not best done by showing, as compatibilists usually try to, that the contrast between 'could have done otherwise' and 'couldn't have done otherwise' still survives if humans are machines. All that is required for responsibility and choice is that things might be otherwise, or that things might have been otherwise. And this is always guaranteed by the logically possible. To put this another way, in your cognitive science parlance, it is the succession of functional states to which blame and praise attach; it is not the means — whether function-ally preemptive, or mechanistic — whereby these functional states are embodied that counts. The solution to the apparent conflict between mechanism and free choice comes through meditation on the amazing spontaneity of even the most rigidly fixed and uniform causal process. "It just happens this way, again and again and again!" When we fully identify with the spontaneity of the regular, then we're no longer tempted by the illusion of a contrastive "I can do this, I can't do that." And it's that contrast which is at the core of any lingering sense of conflict between human mechanism, if it is true, and the making of true choice, or being accountable for one's choices. . . You look as though you still have a question.

P: Yes. Doesn't it get you down, thinking you can do anything, and constantly discovering that you're only human every time! How can you be so cheerful about this situation?

M: How *can* I? Don't tell me I'm talking to the wall once again!

(They both laugh.)

Bibliography

Allen, J.F. (1984). "Towards a General Theory of Action and Time." *Artificial Intelligence*, 23, pp. 123-154.

Anderson, J. (1984). "Cognitive Psychology." *Artificial Intelligence*, 23, pp. 1-11.

Angel, L. (1974). *Recursive Grammars and The Creative Aspect of Language Use.* Ph.D. Thesis, University of British Columbia, Special Collection.

————. (1983). *The Silence of the Mystic.* Philosophy in Canada Monographs.

Anglin, J. (1977). *Word, Object, and Conceptual Development.* New York: W.W. Norton.

Atkinson, M. (1982). *Explanation in the Study of Child Language Development.* Cambridge: Cambridge University Press.

Austin, J.L. (1962). *How to Do Things with Words.* Oxford.

Bennett, J. (1964). *Rationality.* London: Routledge and Kegan Paul.

————. (1976). *Linguistic Behavior.* Cambridge: Cambridge University Press.

Block, N.J. (1978). "Troubles with Functionalism," in C.W. Savage, ed., *Perception and Cognition: Issues in the Foundations of Psychology.* Minneapolis: University of Minnesota Press.

————. (1981). "Psychologism and Behaviorism. *The Philosophical Review*, 90.

Braitenberg, V. (1984). *Vehicles: Experiments in Synthetic Psychology.* Cambridge, MA: MIT Press/A Bradford Book.

Brown, G. (1980). "Action Description in Indirect Speech Acts." *Cognition and Brain Theory*, 3, pp. 82-89.

Brown, R. (1973). *A First Language: The early stages.* Cambridge, Mass: Harvard University Press.

Bruce, B.Q., and D. Newman. (1978). "Interacting Plans." *Cognitive Science*, 2, pp. 195-233.

Carey, S. (1978). "The Child as Word Learner," in M. Halle, J. Blesnan, and G. Miller, eds., *Linguistic Theory and Psychological Reality.* Cambridge, MA: MIT Press.

Charniak, E. (1981). "A Common Representation for Problem-Solving and Language Comprehension Information." *Artificial Intelligence*, 16, pp. 225-255.

Chisholm, R. (1966). "Freedom and Action," in K. Lehrer, ed., *Freedom and Determinism.* New York: Random House.

Churchland, P.S. (1981). "On the Alleged Backwards Referral of Experiences and Its Relevance to the Mind Body Problem." *Philosophy of Science*, 48, pp. 165-181.

————. (1986). *Neurophilosophy: Toward a Unified Theory of Mind/Brain.* Cambridge, MA: MIT Press/A Bradford Book.

Cohen, P., and C. Perrault. (1979). "Elements of a Plan-Based Theory of Speech Acts." *Cognitive Science*, 3, pp. 177-212.

Danto, A.C. (1965). "Basic Actions." *American Philosophical Quarterly*, 2, pp. 141-148.

Davidson, D. (1980). "Agency," in Davidson, D., *Essays on Actions and Events*. Oxford: Clarendon Press.

Davis, L. (1979). *Theory of Action*. Englewood Cliffs, NJ: Prentice-Hall.

Davis, S. (1980). "Perlocutions," in J.R. Searle, F. Kiefer, and M. Bierwisch, eds., *Speech Act Theory and Pragmatics*. Hingham, MA: D. Reidel.

Dennett, D.C. (1969). *Content and Consciousness*. London: Routledge and Kegan Paul.

———. (1978a)."Towards a Cognitive Theory of Consciousness," in *Brainstorms: Philosophical Essays on Mind and Psychology*. Montgomery, VT: Bradford Books.

———. (1978b). "Where Am I?" in Dennett, D., *Brainstorms: Philosophical Essays on Mind and Psychology*. Montgomery, VT: Bradford Books.

———. (1983). *Elbow Room: The Varieties of Free Will Worth Wanting*. Cambridge, MA: MIT Press/A Bradford Book.

de Villiers, J.G., and P.A. de Villiers. (1978). *Language Acquisition*. Cambridge, MA: Harvard University Press.

Dietterich, T.G., and R.S. Michalski. (1981). "Inductive Learning of Structural Descriptions." *Artificial Intelligence*, 16, pp. 257-294.

Dilworth, D., and H. Silverman. (1978). "The De-Ontological Self Paradigm." *The Monist*, 61, 1, pp. 82-95.

Dixon, N. (1981). *Preconscious Processing*. Chichester: John Wiley and Sons.

Dreyfus, H. (1979). *What Computers Can't Do*. New York: Harper Colophon.

Dreyfus, H., and S. Dreyfus. (1986). *Mind over Machine*. New York: Free Press.

Eccles, J. (1976). "Brain and Free Will," in G. Globus, G. Maxwell, and I. Savodnik, eds., *Consciousness and the Brain*. New York: Plenum Press.

Eccles, J. and K. Popper. (1977). *The Self and Its Brain*. Berlin and New York: Springer International.

Eccles J. and D. Robinson. (1985). *The Wonder of Being Human*. Boulder, Co: Shambhala.

Evans, D. (1985). *Situations and Speech Acts*. New York: Garland.

Fingarette, H. (1963). *The Self in Transformation*. New York: Basic Books.

Fodor, J.A. (1975). *The Language of Thought*. Hassocks, Sussex: Harvester Press.

———. (1982a). "Tom Swift and His Procedural Grandmother," in Fodor, J.A., *Representations*. Cambridge, MA: MIT Press/A Bradford Book.

———. (1982b). "Methodological Solipsism Considered as a Research Strategy in Cognitive Psychology," in Fodor, J.A., *Representations*. Cambridge, MA: MIT Press/A Bradford Book.

Frankfurt, H. (1969). "Alternate Possibilities and Moral Responsibility," *Journal of Philosophy*, 65, pp. 829-833.

Gardner, H. (1985). *The Mind's New Science*. New York: Basic Books.

Gert, B. and T. Duggan. (1979). "Free Will as the Ability to Will." *Nous*, 13, pp. 197-217.

Grice, H.P. (1957). "Meaning." *Philosophical Review*, 66, pp. 377-88.

————. (1975). "Method in Philosophical Psychology." *American Philosophical Association Proceedings*, 48, pp. 23-53.

Griffin, D.R. (1984). *Animal Thinking*. Cambridge, MA: Harvard University Press.

Grimshaw, J. (1981). "Form, Function, and the Language Acquisition Device," in C.L. Baker and J. McCarthy, eds., *The Logical Problem of Language Acquisition*. Cambridge, MA: MIT Press.

Gunderson, K. (1971). *Mentality and Machines*. Garden City, NY: Anchor Doubleday.

Gustafson, D. (1986). *Intention and Agency*. Philosopical Studies, No. 33. Hingham, MA: D. Reidel.

Harnad, S. (1982). "Metaphor and Mental Duality," in T. Simon and R. Scholes, eds., *Language, Mind and Brain*. Hillsdale, NJ: Erlbaum.

Hartocollis, P. (1983). *Time and Timelessness*. New York: International Universities Press.

Hobbs, J. and D. Evans. (1980). "Conversation as Planned Behavior," in *Cognitive Science*, 4, pp. 349-377.

Jackendoff, R.S. (1987). *Consciousness and the Computational Mind.*. Cambridge, MA: MIT Press.

Jacobs, W. (1972). "How a Bug's Mind Works," in H.W. Robinson and D.E. Knight, eds., *Cybernetics, Artificial Intelligence and Ecology*. New York: Macmillan Spartan.

Johnson-Laird, P.N. (1983). *Mental Models*. Cambridge, MA: Harvard University Press.

Lehiste, I. (1970). *Suprasegmentals*. Cambridge, MA: MIT Press.

Lem, S. (1974). "The Seventh Sally, or How Trurl's Own Perfection Led to No Good," in S. Lem, *The Cyberiad*, translated by M. Kandel. New York: Seabury Press. (Reprinted in D. Hofstadter and D. Dennett, *The Mind's I: Fantasies and Reflections on Self and Soul*. New York: Basic Books, 1981.)

————. (1978). "Non Serviam," in S. Lem, *A Perfect Vacuum: Perfect Reviews of Nonexistent Books*. New York: Harcourt Brace Jovanovich, Inc. (Reprinted in D. Hofstadter and D. Dennett, *The Mind's I*, 1981.)

Libet, B. (1978). "Neuronal Vs. Subjective Timing for a Conscious Sensory Experience," in P. Buser and A. Rougel-Buser, eds., *Cerebral Correlates of Conscious Experience*. Amsterdam: Elsevier.

————. (1981). "The Experimental Evidence for Subjective Referral of a Sensory Experience Backwards in Time: Reply to P.S. Churchland," in *Philosophy of Science*, 48, pp. 182-197.

Libet, B., and E.W. Wright, B. Feinstein, and D.K. Pearl. (1979). "Subjective Referral of the Timing for a Conscious Sensory Experience," in *Brain*, 102, pp. 193-224.

Lieber, J. (1985). *Can Animals and Machines Be Persons?* Indianapolis, In: Hackett.

Lowenthal, F. (1982). "Can Apes Tell Us What Language Is?" in F. Lowenthal, F. Vandamme, and J. Cordier, eds., *Language and Language Acquisition*. New

York: Plenum Press.

Lycan, W. (1981). "Form, Function and Feel," *Journal of Philosophy*, 78, pp. 24-49.

――――. (1987). *Consciousness*. Cambridge, MA: MIT Press/A Bradford Book.

Mackie, J.L. (1977). "The Grounds of Responsibility," in P.M.S. Hacker and J. Raz, eds., *Law, Morality and Society*. Oxford: Oxford University Press.

Macnamara, J. (1986). *A Border Dispute: The Place of Logic in Psychology*. Cambridge, MA: MIT Press/A Bradford Book.

McGinn, C. (1982). *The Character of Mind*. Oxford: Oxford University Press.

Miller, M. (1979). *The Logic of Language Development in Early Childhood*. Berlin and New Yrok: Springer-Verlag.

Minsky, M., ed. (1985). *Robotics*. Garden City, NJ: Anchor Doubleday.

――――. (1986). *The Society of Mind*. New York: Simon and Schuster.

Nagel, T. (1975). "Brain Bisection and the Unity of Consciousness," in J. Perry, ed., *Personal Identity*. Berkeley: University of California Press.

――――. (1979a). "Panpsychism," in Nagel, T., *Mortal Questions*. Cambridge: Cambridge University Press.

――――. (1979b). "Objective and Subjective," in Nagel, T., *Mortal Questions*. Cambridge: Cambridge University Press.

――――. (1986).*The View From Nowhere*. Oxford: Oxford University Press.

Newson, J. (1978). "Dialogue and Development," in A. Lock, ed., *Action, Gesture, and Symbol*. London and New York: Academic Press.

Pinker, S. (1984). *Language Learnability and Language Development*. Cambridge, MA: Harvard University Press.

Plooij, F.X. (1978). "Some Basic Traits of Language in Wild Chimpanzees," in A. Lock, ed., *Action, Gesture, and Symbol*. London and New York: Academic Press.

Pribram, K., M. Nuwer, and R. Baron. (1974). "The Holographic Hypothesis of Memory Structure," in D.H. Krantz et al., eds., *Contemporary Developments in Mathematical Psychology*,. Vol. 2., San Francisco: W.H. Freeman.

Pylyshyn, Z. (1980). "The 'Causal Power' of Machines." *Behavioural and Brain Sciences*, 3, pp. 442-444.

――――. (1984). *Computation and Cognition: Toward a Foundation for Cognitive Science*. Cambridge, MA: MIT Press/A Bradford Book.

Quine, W.V.O. (1960). *Word and Object*. Cambridge, MA: MIT Press.

Ringle, M. (1982). "Artificial Intelligence and Semantic Theory," in T. Simon and R. Scholes, eds., *Language, Mind, and Brain*. Hillsdale, NJ: Erlbaum.

Sachs, O. (1985). *The Man Who Mistook His Wife for a Hat*. New York: Simon and Shuster.

Salveter, S. (1979). "Inferring Conceptual Graphs," *Cognitive Science*, 3, pp. 141-166.

Schaffer, H.R., ed. (1977). *Studies in Mother Infant-Interaction*. London and New York: Academic Press.

Schank, R., and R. Abelson. (1977). *Scripts, Plans, Goals, and Understanding*. Hillsdale, NJ: Erlbaum.

Schlesinger, I.M. (1982). *Steps to Language*. Hillsdale, NJ: Erlbaum.

Searle, J. (1979). "A Taxonomy of Illocutionary Acts," in J. Searle, *Expression and*

Meaning. Cambridge: Cambridge University Press.

———. (1982). "Minds, Brains and Programs," in J. Haugeland, ed., *Mind Design*. Cambridge, MA: MIT Press / A Bradford Book.

———. (1983). *Intentionality: An Essay in the Philosophy of Mind*. Cambridge: Cambridge University Press.

———. (1984). *Minds, Brains and Science*. London: BBC.

Strawson, P.F. (1959). *Individuals*. London: Methuen.

———. (1968). "Freedom and Resentment," in P.F. Strawson, *Studies in the Philosophy of Thought and Action*. Oxford: Oxford University Press.

Swartz, N. (1985). *The Concept of Physical Law*. Cambridge: Cambridge University Press.

Swinburne, R. (1977). *The Coherence of Theism*. Oxford: Oxford University Press.

Taylor, R. (1966). *Action and Purpose*. Englewood Cliffs, NJ: Prentice-Hall.

Thorp, J. (1980). *Free Will: A Defence Against Neurophysiological Determinism*. London and Boston: Routledge and Kegan Paul.

Trusted, J. (1984). *Free Will and Responsibility*. Oxford: Oxford University Press.

Turing, A.M. (1963). "Computing Machinery and Intelligence," in E. Feigenbaum and F. Feldman, eds., *Computers and Thought*. New York: McGraw Hill.

Turkle, S. (1984). *The Second Self*. New York: Simon and Schuster.

Urwin, C. (1978). "The Development of Communication Between Blind Infants and Their Parents," in A. Lock, ed., *Action, Gesture, and Symbol*. New York: Academic Press.

van Inwagen, P. (1983). *An Essay on Free Will*. Oxford: Clarendon.

Winograd, T. (1972). *Understanding Natural Language*. London and New York: Academic Press.

Winson, J. (1985). *Brain and Psyche: The Biology of the Unconscious*. New York: Vintage.

Wolf, S. (1980). "Asymmetrical Freedom." *Journal of Philosophy*, 67, pp. 151-165.

Index

W. D. Perry